Published 2004 by Grange Books
an imprint of Grange Books PLC.
The Grange
Kings North Industrial Estate
Hoo nr. Rochester
Kent, UK
ME3 9ND
www.grangebooks.co.uk

All enquiries please email info@grangebooks.co.uk

All notations of errors or omissions (author inquiries, permissions) concerning the content of this
book should be addressed to:
TAJ Books 27, Ferndown Gardens, Cobham, Surrey, UK, KT11 2BH, info@tajbooks.com.

ISBN 1-84013-696-0

Printed in China.

1 2 3 4 5 08 07 06 05 04

WORLD WAR I
DAY BY DAY

Alex Hook

Grange
BOOKS

Defining moments: The Somme. From top to bottom: The waiting line is ready to scramble over the top. Two men are immediately shot even before they go to dash into No Man's Land. The first obstacle is the wire which has to be cut — all the while enemy machine-gun and rifle fire find their targets. More men lie dying.

Above: General Erich Ludendorff was a specialist in mobilisation logistics.

Top: Verdun. Midnight mass in an improvised chapel attended by the French defenders of Fort de Douamont.

Right: Queen Mary placing a floral tribute to the dead on the Roll of Honour in Balcorne Street, South Hackney, London.

June 28, 1914, Archduke Franz Ferdinand and his wife, the Duchess of Hohenberg, leave the town hall at Sarajevo. In a short time they will be dead and the inexorable slide to war will start.

1914

June 1914

Tension is already high before the outbreak of war. European countries are enmeshed in a complex series of alliances guaranteeing armed support and involvement should an ally be threatened. In the Balkans hostilities are most tense with Germany and Austria-Hungary contesting power and influence in the region against Russia through their smaller allies Serbia and Bosnia.

28

Politics: The heir to the Austro-Hungarian Empire, Archduke Franz Ferdinand of Austria, is assassinated in Sarajevo, Bosnia by a Serbian Nationalist, Gavrilo Princip. His wife, Sophia the duchess of Hohenberg, also dies. This event triggers the war when a complicated set of alliances rapidly bring most of Europe to mobilization and, subsequently, armed conflict.

29

Politics: Austria-Hungary accuses Serbia of being instrumental in the assassination. Great civil and political unrest in Bosnia and Serbia.

July 1914

Across the Balkans in particular, but in Europe generally, tensions run high as imminent war is anticipated. Britain starts reinforcing its positions on the Suez Canal in anticipation of an attack by Turkey.

4

Politics: Archduke's funeral; the Kaiser does not attend.

6

Politics: Germany promises to support its ally Austria-Hungary in any action it undertakes against Serbia.

Europe rushes to war
JUL

Battle of Frontiers in west; Tannenberg in east
AUG

Invasion of France
SEP

Race to the Sea reaches the Channel
OCT

Trench warfare in west; Mesopotamian Front opens
NOV

Trench warfare in east; Champagne Offensive in west
DEC

Top: German field gun.

Bottom: German light cruisers and destroyers manoeuvre in the Baltic.

17
Politics: Serbia is reported to be preparing for war and calling up 70,000 reserve soldiers.

20
Politics: The Austro-Hungarian army is reported to be mustering along its side of the Serbian border.

23
Politics: Austria-Hungary sends an ultimatum to Serbia, including a demand to arrest and hand over the leaders of the Black Hand within 48 hours. Germany fully supports the demands.

24
Politics: Serbia appeals to its historic ally Russia for help. Russian cabinet proposes international mediation.

25
Politics: Serbia refuses to hand over leaders of the Black Hand group; Crown Prince signs the order for mobilization of troops.
Russia still wants peace but calls up reserves (13 corps) to prepare to mobilize at the Russian-Austrian border.

26
Politics: Germany threatens to mobilize its troops if Russia continues war preparations. Austria mobilizes troops at border with Russia.
Russia is still attempting to broker a peace but makes it clear that it will not stand idly by if Serbia is invaded. Announces Russia will mobilize immediately if Austrian troops cross into Serbia.

The ensuing conflict would be the most destructive of all wars.

28

Politics: Austria-Hungary declares war on Serbia and refuses all offers of mediation. Accuses Serbia of provoking the assassination of Archduke Franz Ferdinand and his wife, but promises that it has no quarrel with Russia.

29

Politics: Russia, as Serbia's ally, orders the mobilization of the southern corps on the Austrian border, but avows no quarrel with Germany.
Germany warns Russia that even partial mobilization will start a war between them.

Eastern Front: The opening salvos of the war occur when the Austro-Hungarian fortress of Zemun bombards Belgrade. Austria-Hungary repeatedly attempts to invade Serbia by crossing the River Danube between Gradishte and Belgrade but is repulsed 18 times.

Western Front: The first German patrols cross the French frontier.

30

Politics: Russia offers to stop mobilizing if Austro-Hungarian threats to Serbian sovereignty are withdrawn.
Germany attempts to get Great Britain, France, and Russia to agree to neutrality.

Western Front: German troops muster close to the French border.

31

Politics: Russia announces general mobilization.
Austria announces general mobilization.
Turkey starts to mobilize troops and agrees a secret pact with Germany.
Germany announces that it is on the brink of war but will stop if Russia ceases all aggression. Germany also insists on a quick

Europe rushes to war
JUL

Battle of Frontiers in west; Tannenberg in east
AUG

Invasion of France
SEP

Race to the Sea reaches the Channel
OCT

Trench warfare in west; Mesopotamian Front opens
NOV

Trench warfare in east; Champagne Offensive in west
DEC

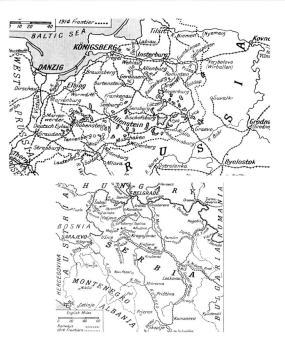

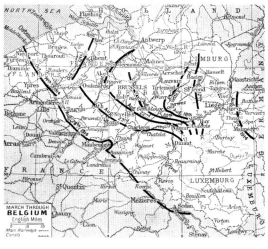

Top: Map of East Prussia showing the terrain over which the Russians advanced in August 1814, and the Masurian Lakes area where they were defeated.

Bottom: Map of Serbia showing area of fighting. Note Sarajevo, where the Archduke was assassinated, at left.

Map showing the German advance line from August 3 to 24, 1914.

answer (within 18 hours) regarding France's position — will she remain neutral?.

The British government refuses to commit to supporting France should it be invaded. The Stock Exchange in London is closed as the situation causes a financial crisis.

As France declares that it will act in its own best interests, the French Socialist leader, M. Jaurès, is assassinated in Paris.

August 1914

The political tension has erupted into open conflict as more and more countries are drawn into open warfare by honoring their treaties. Battle fronts open in the East and the West.

1

Eastern Front: Germany declares war on Russia at 7.10pm blaming Russia (falsely) for crossing the frontier that afternoon and starting the war. Germany orders a general mobilization and demands the neutrality of Russia's ally France and detains British ships in Hamburg.

Politics: France orders general mobilization at 3.40pm.
Belgium declares her neutrality.
Italy announces her neutrality.

2

Eastern Front: Germany invades Poland and occupies Chenstokhov, Bendzin, and Kalish. Russian troops enter Germany near Schwidden.

Belgian troops man a trench.

Politics: Britain pledges to protect French shipping in the English Channel from German aggression.

Western Front: Germany invades Luxembourg and German troops cross the French border at four locations. The first French soldiers are killed near Belfort. Germany demands free passage through Belgium – wants an answer within 12 hours – so that she can attack France.

3

Politics: Germany declares war on France. Belgium rejects Germany's demand for neutrality and free passage: appeals for British help.
Great Britain orders a general mobilization.

4

United States: President Woodrow Wilson makes a Proclamation of Neutrality affirming the already stated U.S. position.

War at sea: German cruisers Goeben and Breslau bombard Bona and Philippeville in Algeria.

Western Front: Following General Moltke's Schlieffen Plan to knock-out France, German troops under General Von Kluck cross the Belgian border at Gemmerich. Halted at Liége. Germany declares war on Belgium.
Great Britain declares she will be at war with Germany at 11pm. Lord Kitchener becomes Secretary of War. Sir John Jellicoe takes command of the British Fleet.

5

Politics: Austria-Hungary declares war on Russia.

United States: President Wilson offers his mediation services in the interests of peace.

Europe rushes to war
JUL

Battle of Frontiers in west; Tannenberg in east
AUG

Invasion of France
SEP

Race to the Sea reaches the Channel
OCT

Trench warfare in west; Mesopotamian Front opens
NOV

Trench warfare in east; Champagne Offensive in west
DEC

Belgian troops in battle.

The area around Liege showing its forts.

War at sea: German minelayer Königen Luise sunk by cruiser HMS Amphion and destroyers off Harwich. HMS Lance is thought to have fired the first shots of the war at sea.

Western Front: In Belgium the Battle of Liege sees the fall of Fort Fléron.

6

War at sea: HMS Amphion is sunk by Königen Luise's mines in the North Sea.

Western Front: Around Liege more forts fall to the Germans: Big Bertha (gun) is used against the Liege forts.

7

Eastern Front: The First Russian Army under Rennenkampf crosses into East Prussia.

Politics: Montenegro declares war with Austria.

Western Front: First members of the British Expeditionary Force (BEF) land in France at Ostend, Calais and Dunkirk to help defend against the German invasion.
Lord Kitchener calls for 100,000 men to join British Army
General Joffre as supreme commander of the French army orders the invasion of Alsace.
Start of the Battle of Mulhouse as the French Army cross the border into Alsace.

8

Balkans: Austrian fleet bombards Antivari in Montenegro.
Serbia at war with Germany.

Politics: Switzerland mobilizes and declares a state of siege.

Western Front: Belgian army retreats as the Germans advance.

The Russian Tsar accompanied by Grand-Duke Nicholas salutes as he inspects his troops.

9

War at sea: First German submarine loss of the war: U-15 sunk by HMS Birmingham off Fair Isle.

10

Africa: From South-West Africa German soldiers raid into Cape Colony.

Eastern Front: Austrian First Army invades Russian Poland and advances towards Lyublin and Kyeltsi.

Politics: France declares war on Austria-Hungary.

War at sea: Turkey allows the German Mittelmeer division under Admiral Souchon into her terrritorial waters with the battlecruiser Goeben and the light cruiser Breslau.

Western Front: Liege is captured by the Germans.
French invade Lorraine under the leadership of General de Castelnau.

11

Politics: Great Britain declares war on Austria-Hungary.

War at sea: German ships Goeben and Breslau enter the Dardanelles and are soon reported to have been bought by the Turks.

Western Front: Fierce fighting continues in Belgium.

12

Balkans: Austro-Hungarian troops invade Serbia.

Politics: Montenegro declares war against Germany.

Europe rushes to war
JUL

Battle of Frontiers in west; Tannenberg in east
AUG

Invasion of France
SEP

Race to the Sea reaches the Channel
OCT

Trench warfare in west; Mesopotamian Front opens
NOV

Trench warfare in east; Champagne Offensive in west
DEC

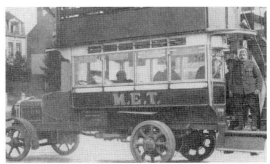

Right bottom: B type London bus carrying British wounded from Antwerp to Ghent.

Top: Belgian troops at a field kitchen.

Western Front: Battle of Haelen in Belgium on the Belgian Army's first line of defense.

13

Africa: In Tanganiyka (German East Africa) British forces raid and bombard the port of Dar-es-Salaam.

Western Front: Under the command of Brig-Gen David Henderson, Nos. 2, 3, 4, and 5 Squadrons of the Royal Flying Corps (RFC), deploy to France in support of the BEF between 13 and 15 August.

14

Balkans: Austria occupies Loznitsa in Serbia.

Western Front: Battle of the Frontiers begins as French General Joffre launches an invasion of Germany through Lorraine.

15

Eastern Front: The Russian invasion of East Prussia begins.

Far East: Japanese send an ultimatum to Germany demanding the evacuation of Tsingtao in China.

General: The Panama Canal opens to traffic for the first time.

16

Western Front: The first contingent of the BEF is now in France.

17

Balkans: The Battle of the Jadar starts; it ends on the 19th with the Austrians routed by the Serbs who press the Austrians into flight across the border.

German Army marching through Belgium 1914.

Eastern Front: Start of the Battle of Stallupönen in East Prussia that ends on 19th with defeat the Germans by the Russians.

Western Front: Belgian capital removed from Brussels to Antwerp.

18
Eastern Front: Russian troops under Brusilov and Russki start the invasion of eastern Galicia: they make fast progress.

19
Politics: The United States of America declares its neutrality.
The Canadian Parliament authorises the raising of an expeditionary force to send overseas. Valcartier Camp is constructed to give basic training to new recruits.

Western Front: Maubeuge, Belgium: first RFC reconnaissance flight made in a Blériot of No 3 Sqn and a BE2 of No 4 Sqn.

20
Eastern Front: Battle of Gumbinnen in East Prussia is won by Russia.

General: In Rome Pope Pius X dies.

Western Front: German soldiers occupy Brussels.
The French are driven back from Lorraine during the Battle of the Frontiers.

21
Africa: South Africa is invaded by German troops.

Western Front: Battle of the Ardennes as the invading armies of Germany and France clash in the forests of the lower Ardennes. One of the most important of the series of battles known as 'The Battles of the Frontiers.'

Europe rushes to war
JUL

Battle of Frontiers in west; Tannenberg in east
AUG

Invasion of France
SEP

Race to the Sea reaches the Channel
OCT

Trench warfare in west; Mesopotamian Front opens
NOV

Trench warfare in east; Champagne Offensive in west
DEC

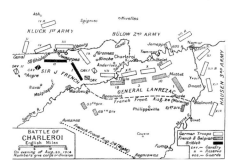

Top: Battle of Charleroi on evening of August 23, 1914.
Bottom: Germans captured by the French.

German Uhlans using a cart drawn by dogs.

Start of the Battle of Charleroi (between Mons and the Meuse) between French and German troops. The British move towards Mons to support their allies.
As the Siege of Namur continues the Belgians are forced to abandon their trenches.

22

Western Front: Belgians start the evacuation of Namur. French are suffering defeats as the Germans advance.
RFC reconnaissance detects a German attempt to envelope allied troops.
German troops massacre 400 Belgian civilians at Tamines.

23

Eastern Front: Hindenburg and Ludendorff given command of the German Eastern Front. In East Prussia the Germans are driven back at the Battle of Frankenau. Austria-Hungary invades Galicia (Russian Poland).

Far East: Japan declares war on Germany. Begin attack on Tsingtao with a bombardment and blockade.

Western Front: The start of the Battle of Mons. The BEF is massively outnumbered by the attacking Germans but manages to slow their advance.
Fall of Namur.

24

Western Front: British and French retreat in a line from the Sambre to the Meuse.
The BEF starts to withdraw from Mons.
Germans enter France near Lille. French civilians are massacred at Dinant.

Improvised German band in Poland.

25

Africa: Tepe in the Cameroons is occupied by the Allies.

Balkans: In Serbia the first Austrian invasion ends with the Austrians sustaining heavy losses.

Eastern Front: In Poland the Russians are defeated at Krasnik by the Austrian First Army.

Politics: Austria-Hungary declares war with Japan.

Western Front: The BEF in full retreat from Mons.
Start of the siege of Maubeuge; Sédan is captured; the line of Le Cateau-Esnes is overrun by the Germans.
The RFC's first enemy aircraft is brought down after three BE2 aircraft of 2 Sqn force it to crash land. Aircraft are not yet armed but the crews were issued with guns or revolvers.

26

Eastern Front: Battle of Tannenberg in East Prussia begins. German troops destroy the invading Russians and halt their advance into East Prussia. This is Germany's greatest success of the war on Eastern Front.

Politics: Viviani becomes premier of France.

War at sea: German cruiser Magdeburg runs aground in the Baltic and the Russians seize a copy of the German naval codebook.

Western Front: Battle of Le Cateau: BEF is forced to retreat.

27

Politics: Austria declares war on Belgium.

Europe rushes to war
JUL

Battle of Frontiers in west; Tannenberg in east
AUG

Invasion of France
SEP

Race to the Sea reaches the Channel
OCT

Trench warfare in west; Mespotamian Front opens
NOV

Trench warfare in east; Champagne Offensive in west
DEC

Top: German troops in a defensive position during the battle of Tannenberg in East Prussia.

Bottom: BEF 60-pounder.

Western Front: Germans occupy Lille and Mézières. British abandon St Quentin.

War at sea: At sea HMS Highflyer sinks Kaiser Wilhelm der Grosse. While in the Gulf of Finland the German cruiser Magdeburg is destroyed.

28

Eastern Front: At Lützow in Galicia the Germans are beaten by the Russians.

War at sea: Battle of Heligoland Bight. Sir David Beatty sends Harwich Force — light cruisers, Fearless and Arethusa and 25 destroyers — to raid Heligoland base and attack German patrols. The German light cruisers Ariadne, Mainz, Köln and destroyer V.187 are sunk. Around 1,000 sailors are lost. The flagship HMS Arethusa is badly damaged but towed to safety.

Royal Marines landed at Ostend August 27-28, 1914.

Western Front: Fall of Longwy, on the Luxembourg border.

29

Eastern Front: Battle of Tannenburg in East Prussia between Von Hindenburg's German army and Samsonov's invading Second Army ends in the rout of the Russians.

Pacific: In Samoa soldiers from New Zealand occupy German holdings.

Western Front: Start of the Battle of Guise (aka Battle of Guise-St. Quentin): a counter-attack by the French Fifth Army as it retreated along the River Oise.
French and BEF forces fight fierce retreats. The latter to the Compiègne-Soissons line.

30

Africa: In the Cameroons the British occupy Nsanakong.

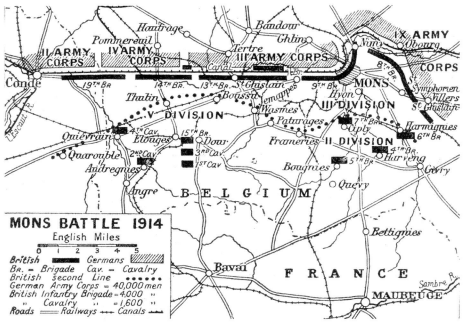

Battle of Mons, August 22, 1914.

Eastern Front: The Germans capture many retreating Russian soldiers fallowing the end of the Battle of Tannenburg.

Western Front: Laon occupied by Germans. Paris is bombed by Germans for the first time.

31
Eastern Front: General Alexander Samsonov becomes German prisoner. Rennenkampf forced to retreat back to the Russian border.

Western Front: Start of the Battle of the Grande Couronne of Nancy.

September 1914
The 'Race to the Sea' begins on the Western Front as a means of out-flanking each other, both sides attempt to control the sea ways and the Channel ports. On the Eastern Front, attempted invasions of Galicia, East Prussia, and Serbia all fail.

1
Eastern Front: Austrians lose at the Battle of Lemberg (Lvov) in Galicia.
Front lines have appeared to the north and east of Stanislau.

General: In Russia St. Petersburg is renamed Petrograd.

Western Front: Soissons comes under heavy German bombardment.

2
Eastern Front: Following defeat at the Battle of Lemberg (Lvov) the Austro-Hungarians lose 130,000 men.

Far East: Japanese troops land at Lungkow to start besieging the German fortress colony of Tsingtao.

Europe rushes to war **JUL**

Battle of Frontiers in west; Tannenberg in east **AUG**

Invasion of France **SEP**

Race to the Sea reaches the Channel **OCT**

Trench warfare in west; Mesopotamian Front opens **NOV**

Trench warfare in east; Champagne Offensive in west **DEC**

Map showing the terrain over which the British Army retreated from Mons to the River Marne, including Le Cateau where Smith-Dorrien's 2nd Corps stood.

Troops after the attack on Tsingtao.

Western Front: The French government abandons Paris and transfers to Bordeaux; about 500,000 people also flee Paris.

3

Eastern Front: The capital of Galicia, Lemberg (Lvov), is occupied and looted by the Russians.

War at sea: Cruiser Pathfinder sunk by U.21 off Firth of Forth with the loss of 256 lives. HMS Speedy is destroyed by a mine.

Western Front: The advancing Germans reach the River Marne. They hold a line across norhtern France from Château Thierry-River Suippe-Ville sur Tourbe.
As the German cavalry advance to within eight miles of Paris the city is placed in a state of siege.

4

Eastern Front: Russians set up a provisional government in Galicia.

Western Front: As the Germans advance on Antwerp the Belgians open the dykes to flood the land.

5

Eastern Front: In Poland the Russians defeat the Austrians at Tomashov.
Brusilov's Army captures Mikolajow in the Carpathians.

Politics: In London Britain, Russia, and France sign The Agreement of London vowing not to seek separate peace.

War at sea: Cruiser HMS Pathfinder is sunk by U-boat U-21 as she leaves Rosyth harbor. The Wilson liner Runo is blown up by a mine. In East Africa the Germans attack Abercorn.

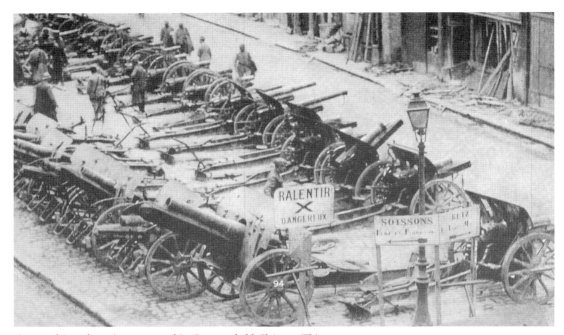

Captured French equipment stored in German-held Château-Thierry.

Western Front: Battle of the Ourcq — Maunoury's Sixth Army.
Germans capture Rheims and Pont-à-Mousson. Germany now finds that she is committed to fighting a war on two fronts.

6

Africa: In the Cameroons British soldiers suffer a reverse near Nsanakong.

Balkans: Serbia invades Syrmia.

Eastern Front: Battle of Grodek southwest of Lemberg (Lvov).

Western Front: The Allies stop retreating and stand firm to halt the German advance at the First Battle of Marne north-east of Paris. The French 6th Army under General Michel-Joseph Maunoury attack German forces advancing on the capital Paris is saved from the advancing Germans but the upshot is stalemate and trench warfare. Eventually Von Kluck is beaten by General Joffre, and the German army retreats to the Soissons-Rheims. During the course of the battle over two million soldiers will be involved and 100,000 killed or wounded but France was saved from the rapid conquest envisioned by the Schlieffen Plan.
The German army reaches the town of Provins 46 miles southeast of Paris — the most southerly point they achieve.

7

Balkans: Second Austrian invasion of Serbia.

Eastern Front: The Russian cavalry reaches the Carpathians.
First Battle of the Masurian Lakes in East Prussia: first German offensive on the Eastern Front to stop the Russians invading.

War at sea: The Nürnberg manages to cut the

Europe rushes to war
JUL

Battle of Frontiers in west; Tannenberg in east
AUG

Invasion of France
SEP

Race to the Sea reaches the Channel
OCT

Trench warfare in west; Mespotamian Front opens
NOV

Trench warfare in east; Champagne Offensive in west
DEC

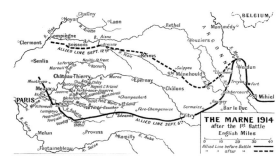

Top: Cavalry anticipate a breakthrough.
Bottom: The "Old Contemptibles" in Belgium, 1914.

Pacific cable between Banfield and Fanning Island.

Western Front: During the Battle of the Marne the Germans capture Maubeuge taking many prisoners.

8

War at sea: Cruiser HMS Oceanic is wrecked off the north coast of Scotland.

Western Front: General Foch forces the Germans back over the Marne. Troyon is bombarded.

9

Balkans: Montenegro invades Bosnia.

Eastern Front: Start of the First Battle of the Masurian Lakes.

Western Front: Battle of Fère Champenoise.

Top: Map showing the battle of the Marne between 6 and 12 September; the battle saved Paris and halted the German advance.

Start of the Great Retreat when German troops retreat back to the River Aisne chased by the BEF; the German commander, Moltke, is replaced by Falkenhayn.

10

Balkans: In Syrmia the Serbians occupy Semlin.

Eastern Front: Second Battle of Krasnik in Poland. Dankl is defeated.

Western Front: Germans abandon Pont-à-Mousson.

11

Pacific: In the Bismarck Archipelago an Australian expedition captures Herbertshöhe.

Western Front: French start to recover lost territory and towns.

French troops on the Aisne.

12

Africa: In East Africa the Germans are defeated near Kisi.

Eastern Front: In Galicia the Russians win the Battle of Grodek and Rava Russka. They capture Grodek and the Austro-Hungarians are utterly defeated.

Western Front: Belgian resistance threatens to cut German communications.
The seige of Troyon is raised by the Germans. Start of the First Battle of the Aisne when French troops attack the German Army at the River Aisne. During this battle the RFC makes its first operational use of aerial photography. The 'Race to the Sea' begins as both sides attempt to outflank each other northeast toward the North Sea coastline.

13

Eastern Front: Russians win a victory at Sredniki in East Prussia when they turn and fight unexpectedly.

Far East: The Japanese capture the railroad at Kiaochau in Tsingtao.

Pacific: In the Solomon Islands Australian troops capture Bougainville.

War at sea: Old German cruiser Hela sunk by British submarine E.9 (Max Horton) six miles southwest of Heligoland island.

Western Front: Amiens and Soissons recovered by the Allies from German occupation.
Fighting along the Aerschot-Malines lines in Belgium.

14

Africa: In South Africa the Germans are defeated at Raman's Drift.

Europe rushes to war
JUL

Battle of Frontiers in west; Tannenberg in east
AUG

Invasion of France
SEP

Race to the Sea reaches the Channel
OCT

Trench warfare in west; Mespotamian Front opens
NOV

Trench warfare in east; Champagne Offensive in west
DEC

Top: BEF artillery heads for a new position.

Below: Early British trench during the battle of the Aisne.

Map showing the first battle of the Aisne.

Balkans: In Bosnia Serbs and Montenegrins take Vishegrad.

Eastern Front: End of the First Battle of the Masurian Lakes.

War at sea: Cap Trafalgar is sunk off the east coast of South America by HMS Carmania.

Western Front: First Battle of Aisne begins with heavy fighting around Vailly and Missy. French reoccupy Amiens and Rheims.

15

Balkans: In Serbia the Austrian second invasion is recalled when they are pushed back over the Drina.

Western Front: Trenches are dug for the first time on the Western Front.
At the Aisne the Germans counter attack and start a slow advance which continues until 21 October. This push is known as the 'Race to the sea.'.
The Germans occupy Arras and bombard Soissons.
For the first time, the RFC makes use of wireless telegraphy during observation flights over enemy artillery positions.

16

Western Front: The Germans take Valenciennes.

17

Eastern Front: Austro-German attack western Poland.

19

Western Front: Heavy fighting on the Western Front continues. .

Belgian troops; note dogs used to pull MGs.

20

Eastern Front: In East Prussia the Germans siege Osovyets.

War at sea: In the Indian Ocean off the isalnd of Zanzibar HMS Pegasus is disabled by the German cruiser Königsberg.

Western Front: Reims cathedral is bombarded by the Germans.

21

Eastern Front: The Russians take Jaroslav and advance towards and start the first siege of Przemysl. The siege lasts until 3 October.

War at sea: In French Tahiti Papeete is bombarded by Scharnhorst and Gneisenau. Allied shipping in the Bay of Bengal is severely disrupted by German naval activity and the Indian port of Madras is bombarded by the cruiser Emden.

British armoured cruisers Aboukir, Hogue, Cressy sunk by U.9 (Weddigen) off Dutch coast with the loss of 1,460.

Western Front: The French retake Noyon and push forward in an attempt to turn the German right wing.

24

Africa: In New Guinea Australlian troops occupy the German town of Friedrich Wilhelm.

Far East: The British join Japanese troops in Tsingtao.

Western Front: The Battle of the Aisne reaches stalemate.
Germans occupy Péronne.

25

Eastern Front: Hindenburg is given command

Europe rushes to war
JUL

Battle of Frontiers in west; Tannenberg in east
AUG

Invasion of France
SEP

Race to the Sea reaches the Channel
OCT

Trench warfare in west; Mespotamian Front opens
NOV

Trench warfare in east; Champagne Offensive in west
DEC

The glorious Gothic cathedral at Reims, where for centuries kings of France were crowned, was badly damaged by German bombing.

Primitive French unarmed reconaissance monoplane.

of the combined Austro-Hungarian and German offensives in Galicia and Poland.

Western Front: Start of the First Battle of Albert as the Germans attempt to thwart the Allies plans to surround them.

26
Eastern Front: Fierce fighting on the Eastern Front leads to the two-day Battle of the Niemen.

Western Front: Germans start the siege of Antwerp by bombarding the city.
Indian soldiers land at the French port of Marseilles to join the fighting.

27
Eastern Front: In Galicia the Russians advance towards Cracow.

Western Front: Germans occupy Malines.

28
Eastern Front: Russian cavalry raid into Hungary.

Western Front: End of the Battle of the Aisne — 14 days of intense fighting.

29
Eastern Front: Germans raise the siege of Osovyets after nine days.

Far East: The Japanese bombard Tsingtao, sinking a German trawler in the harbor.

War at sea: Foreign trawlers are banned from British east coast ports.

Western Front: Germans lose the Battle of Albert which ends after five days.
Antwerp still under intense siege.

Indian troops disembark at Marseilles before being moved to the Western Front.

October 1914

On the Western Front the battle lines reach the English Channel and there is fierce fighting all month. Turkey suddenly sides with the Central Powers and attacks Russian ports on the Black Sea. There is fighting in both South and East Africa. Canadian troops join the Western Front.

1

Eastern Front: Battle of Augustovo starts as Russians attack retreating Germans in east Prussia.

Great Britain: The first division of Canadian troops set sail to complete training in Britain.

Western Front: Germans fail to break the French line around Roye.
First Battle of Arras starts.

2

Africa: British victory in East Africa at Gazi.

War at sea: HMS Cumberland captures nine German ships in Cameroon River.
British Admiralty announces its intention to plant defensive minefields in parts of the North Sea.

3

Eastern Front: Austro-German invade Poland with the intention of capturing Warsaw.
German officers are given command over Austro-Hungarian forces.

Western Front: Germans occupy Ypres.
The outer defenses of Antwerp fall.

4

Balkans: In Bosnia the Serbs and Montenegrins are driven out of the Sarajevo region.

Europe rushes to war
JUL

Battle of Frontiers in west; Tannenberg in east
AUG

Invasion of France
SEP

Race to the Sea reaches the Channel
OCT

Trench warfare in west; Mesopotamian Front opens
NOV

Trench warfare in east; Champagne Offensive in west
DEC

German generals and the Kaiser.

Eastern Front: Joint German and Austro-Hungarian advance towards Russia.

Western Front: Germans make rapid progress towards the coast, sweeping up a number of cities and towns along the way.
Lille under bombardment.

5

Western Front: First German aircraft shot down by Allied plane.
Three British naval brigades reach Antwerp as the Germans win more ground.

6

Eastern Front: Across Poland and Galicia the Russian fall back due to the force of the German push.

Western Front: British troops land at Zeebrugge and Ostend. Arras takes a heavy pounding from the German bombardment.

Top: The Etonians Officers' Training Corps provided a constant supply of officers to the army.

Belgian women distributing walnuts to troops during the defence of Antwerp.

7

Western Front: Start of the evacuation of Antwerp.
Belgian government moves from Antwerp to Ostend.
Germans cross the River Scheldt threatening the Allies retreat.

Far East: Japanese occupy the Marshall Islands in the Pacific Ocean.

8

Western Front: General Foch takes supreme command of all Allied forces defending the west coast.
The evacuation continues as Antwerp is bombarded. Belgian troops and British naval brigades leave 2,000 men captured and interned in the Netherlands.

The Germans took Ypres on October 3. This aerial photo shows the damage that would be done to the city over the next four years. In the centre are the remains of the cathedral and Cloth Hall.

War at sea: At the mouth of the River Ems the British submarine E.9 sinks the German destroyer S.126.

9

Africa: In South Africa anti-British Boers led by Manie Maritz rebel and declare South African independence and war against Britain. 10,000 Boers will join him.

Eastern Front: The Battle of Augustovo ends with the defeat of the Germans.

Western Front: Antwerp surrenders to Germans.
Allied airmen raid the German Zeppelin sheds in Düsseldorf.

10

Eastern Front: In Poland the Germans occupy Lodz.

Western Front: Lille bombarded again.

11

Eastern Front: Russians have big set-backs on the Eastern Front losing Jaroslav, being forced to raise the unsuccessful siege of Przemysl both in Galicia, and losing Sochaczew in Poland.

War at sea: In the Baltic a German submarine sinks the Russian cruiser Pallada.

Western Front: Beginning of the Battle of Flanders – essentially a struggle for who has control of the western coast of Europe.

12

Africa: In South Africa martial law is declared in an attempt to control the constitutional crisis.

Western Front: The Allies evacuate Ostend

Europe rushes to war
JUL

Battle of Frontiers in west; Tannenberg in east
AUG

Invasion of France
SEP

Race to the Sea reaches the Channel
OCT

Trench warfare in west; Mesopotamian Front opens
NOV

Trench warfare in east; Champagne Offensive in west
DEC

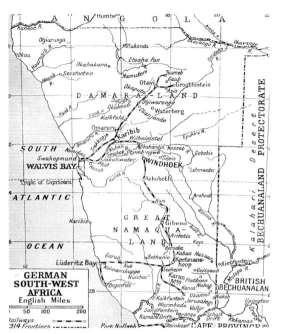

Map showing the area fought over in German Southwest Africa.

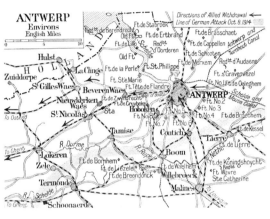

The environs of Antwerp and the German attack of October 8, 1914.

and Zeebrugge as the Germans advance. Germans retreat from Reims.

13

Africa: In South Africa Lt-Col Maritz leads an open rebellion against the British.

Western Front: British occupy Ypres.
Lille and Ghent occupied by the Germans.
Heavy fighting between La Bassée and Bethune.
British receive a copy of the German naval codebook seized from the Magdeburg.
The Belgian government moves again: to Le Havre.
Germany fines the city of Antwerp £20,000,000 for its resistance.

14

Great Britain: The first Canadian troops — 32,000 men of the Canadian Expeditionary Force — arrive in England at Plymouth.

Western Front: Germans occupy Bruges.

15

Africa: In South Africa the rebels are defeated at Ratedraai.

Eastern Front: Start of first Battle for Warsaw.

Far East: Fighting continues in Tsingtao: non-combatants are allowed to leave.

War at sea: In the North Sea the cruiser HMS Hawke is sunk off Peterhead by U.9 500 lost.

Western Front: Germans occupy Ostend and Zeebrugge.

16

Eastern Front: As Germans advance on Warsaw the Russians prepare to evacuate.

German light cruisers manoeuvre in the Baltic.

War at sea: Cattaro is bombarded by Allied warships.
HMS Yarmouth sinks the Emden's collier.

Western Front: The Battle of Yser begins with a German attack on Dixmude.
Allies capture Neuve Chapelle, Aubers, Armentières, and Warneton.

17

Eastern Front: In Poland Russian reinforcements reach Warsaw in time to save the city from the Germans.

War at sea: Off the Dutch coast four German destroyers are sunk by HMS Undaunted and her destroyers.

Western Front: End of the Allied offensive as massive German counter attacking forces them onto the defensive.

18

Western Front: Yser holds out against the Germans with the help of British monitors commanded by Admiral Hood. British submarine E.3 is lost.

19

Western Front: The BEF has now completed its move from Aisne to Flanders.
First Battle of Ypres starts. Ultimately the battle stops the Germans from reaching the English Channel.

20

Eastern Front: Balance of power shifts in the battle for Warsaw as the Russians gain the upper hand.

Western Front: Fierce fighting around Arras. The Cavalry, Meerut and Lahore Division of the Indian Expeditionary Force reach the fighting on the Western Front.

Europe rushes to war
JUL

Battle of Frontiers in west; Tannenberg in east
AUG

Invasion of France
SEP

Race to the Sea reaches the Channel
OCT

Trench warfare in west; Mesopotamian Front opens
NOV

Trench warfare in east; Champagne Offensive in west
DEC

Top: German scouts on the Polish border.
Bottom: German heavy artillery in Poland.

French hospital train from Arras, October 1914.

Germany claims the numbers of prisoners taken are: 9,000 British, 149,000 French, 32,000 Belgian, 107,000 Russian.

21
Eastern Front: The Battle of Kasimiryev: Russians destroy German units east of the Vistula. Germans fall back from Warsaw.

Western Front: Dixmude and Arras suffer under heavy bombardments.
The French start to recover in the Argonne.

22
Western Front: Fierce fighting continues on the Western Front as Germans start a 10-day push to break through Allied lines. Battle around La Bassée.

23
Eastern Front: The Russians are prevailing on the Eastern Front, retaking Jaroslav and forcing the Germans to abandon the siege of Ivangorod.
Polish Legion reaches Nadworna.

24
Africa: In South Africa open rebellion is proving problematic for the government.

Western Front: Fighting around Arras is intense.

25
Eastern Front: In Poland the Germans are in full retreat from advancing Russians. General von Moltke is replaced by General von Falkenhayn.

Western Front: First British aircraft carrier raid attempted on Cuxhaven Zeppelin sheds. Stopped by bad weather.

31

London General Omnibus Company extends its services to France and takes troops towards the front.

26

Africa: In the Cameroons the Allied forces occupy Duala.

Western Front: The German advance is halted along the Yser.
Fierce fighting continues around Ypres, Arras, and La Bsssée.

27

Eastern Front: In Poland the Russian celebrate a victory against the Germans along the Petrokov-Radom line.

Western Front: Germans take Neuve-Chapelle.

War at sea: The Emden captures the Japanese ship Kamasaka Maru.
Admiral Gateaume, a French liner, is sunk.
Dreadnought HMS Audacious sunk by mines left by auxiliary cruiser Berlin, off Lough Swilly, on the coast of Northern Ireland.

28

Eastern Front: In Galicia the Austrians are defeated at Sambor.
In Poland the Russians retake Lodz.

War at sea: Near Penang the Emden sinks the Russian cruiser Zhemchug and other shipping.

Western Front: BEF retake Neuve-Chapelle.

29

Great Britain: Lord Fisher is appointed First Sea Lord of the Royal Navy.

War at sea: Turkey actively joins the Central Power when its ships attack the Russian ports of Odessa, Theodosia, and Novorossisk on the Black Sea.

Western Front: Belgians open the sluices on the canals around Yser to hinder the German attacks.

JUL Europe rushes to war

AUG Battle of Frontiers in west; Tannenberg in east

SEP Invasion of France

OCT Race to the Sea reaches the Channel

NOV Trench warfare in west; Mesopotamian Front opens

DEC Trench warfare in east; Champagne Offensive in west

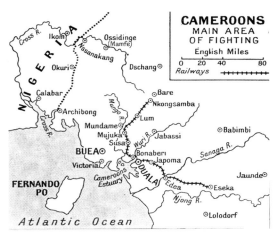

Top: Sir John French and General Joffre in Calais for a conference.
Bottom: German assault led by flamethrowers.

Main areas of fighting in the Cameroons.

30
Africa: In East Africa the Königsberg is discovered hiding in the Rufiji River.

Eastern Front: In Poland the Germans are beaten at Bakalaryevo.

Western Front: Flooding around Yser forces the German soldiers back.

31
War at sea: The British cruiser HMS Hermes is sunk in the Straits of Dover.

Western Front: At Ypres the British line breaks but recovers to retake Gheluvelt. French retake Ramschapelle.

November 1914
Western Front battles start to stagnate as the trenches are dug. The war starts to spread around the world, there is confrontation in the Pacific and Far East and a new front opens up around Mesopotamia and the Caucasus.

1
War at sea: In the Pacific off the coast of Chile a Royal Navy squadron is defeated by German ships led by Vice-Admiral Graf Maximilian von Spee at the Battle of Coronel. HMSs Monmouth and Good Hope are sunk with the loss of 1,600 sailors.

Western Front: Germans capture Messines, Wyteschaete, and Hollebeke.

2
Eastern Front: Russian troops return to East Prussia in the Second Invasion of Prussia.

Politics: Russia declares war on Turkey.

33

All along the Belgian coast German troops had to drag guns and limber over soft sand dunes to get them into position.

Western Front: Germans abandon their Yser positions to concentrate their forces on Ypres. They reoccupy Neuve-Chapelle.

3

Balkans: Montenegrins bombard Cattaro.

Caucasus: Russians advance and occupy Bayazid.

Politics: Serbia declares war on Turkey. Bulgaria declares neutrality.

Western Front: Allies occupy abandoned German positions around Yser.

War at sea: British and French ships bombard Dardanelles forts. On the Red Sea the British first bombard then occupy Aqaba. German battlecruisers bombard the port of Yarmouth and lay offensive mines. During the fight the British submarine D.5 is lost.

4

Africa: In German East Africa German troops rout British-commanded Indian forces at the Battle of Tanga.

Eastern Front: In Galicia the Austrians lose at Jaroslav after 12 days of fighting. 19,000 prisoners are taken.

Politics: Persia refuses to join Turkey and the Central Powers.

War at sea: Returning German armoured cruiser Yorck sunk by own mines in the Jade estuary, Wilhelmshaven.

5

Politics: Turkey joins the Central Powers; Great Britain and France declare war on Turkey.
Great Britain declares war on Turkey.
Cyprus annexed by Britain.

Europe rushes to war
JUL

Battle of Frontiers in west; Tannenberg in east
AUG

Invasion of France
SEP

Race to the Sea reaches the Channel
OCT

Trench warfare in west; Mespotamian Front opens
NOV

Trench warfare in east; Champagne Offensive in west
DEC

Russian infantry in Galicia

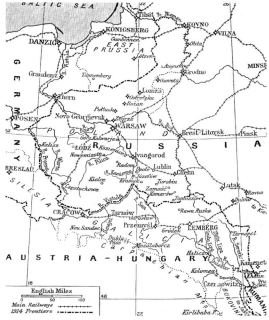

Map showing Galicia and Poland.

British Admiralty declares the North Sea a wholly military area.

6

Far East: In Tsingtao Japanese and British forces capture the central fort and take 200 prisoners.

7

Far East: Japanese capture Tsingtao and take 2,300 prisoners.

Mesopotamia: British forces land in the Persian Gulf.

War at sea: Russian ships bombard Turkish ports on the Black Sea coast.

Western Front: Fierce German attacks at Givenchy and Arras, but repulsed at Roye and Vimy.

8

Balkans: Third Austrian invasion of Serbia starts.

Mesopotamia: British forces occupy Fao on the Persian Gulf.

War at sea: In the Black Sea Russian guns sink four Turkish transports.

Western Front: French advance in Argonne. Still fierce fighting along the Western Front.

9

Caucasus: Battle of Koprukeui in Armenia holds up Russian advance in Caucasus.

Western Front: Determined German assault on British lines at Ypres.

War at sea: Off Cocos Island HMAS Sydney sinks the Emden.

The German raider Emden was caught off the Cocos by Sydney and destroyed.

At Honolulu in the Hawaiian Islands the USA intern the German cruiser Geier.
In East Africa the Königsberg is trapped in the Rufiji River.

11

Balkans: Monetnegrins defeated at the Bosnian frontier at Grahovo.

Eastern Front: Russians begin second siege of Przemysl.

Politics: Turkey formally declares war against the Allies.

Mesopotamia: In the Persian Gulf British forces are attacked at Saniya.

War at sea: HMS Niger is sunk by a German submarine.

Western Front: At Ypres the British lose some trenches to the Prussians but quickly recover them.

14

Eastern Front: Beginning of massive German invasion along the Vistula in Poland.

15

Balkans: Serbs fall back as the Austrians advance.

Eastern Front: Retreating Russians retrench on the Gombin-Lodz line.

Western Front: Last great German attack – by the Prussian Guards – at Ypres fails.

16

Politics: Encouraged by Germany the Turkish sultan calls on all Muslims to rise in jihad (holy war) against British, French and Russian authority.

Europe rushes to war
JUL

Battle of Frontiers in west; Tannenberg in east
AUG

Invasion of France
SEP

Race to the Sea reaches the Channel
OCT

Trench warfare in west; Mesopotamian Front opens
NOV

Trench warfare in east; Champagne Offensive in west
DEC

Indian troops at Basra waiting to join the Mesopotamian expedition. In total India would send over 600,000 men to fight the Turks.

German troops using machine guns in open country as they slowly creep forward.

Western Front: Heavy rain and flooding stop fighting along the Yser.

17

Eastern Front: In Poland fierce fighting between Russians and Austrians around Plotsk.

18

Eastern Front: In East Prussia the Russians are defeated at Soldau.

War at sea: German auxiliary cruiser Berlin runs out of coal, enters andis then interned at Trondheim. In the Black Sea a Russian squadron engages with the Goeben and Breslau. The former sustains damage. On the Baltic, Libau is shelled by a German squadron.

Map of Mesopotamia showing the land between the rivers Tigris and Euphrates.

20

Middle East: In Egypt the Turks advance toward Port Said but are beaten back by the Bakanir Camel Corps.

21

Mesopotamia: Anglo-Indian invasion of Mesopotamia occupies Basra to protect the flow of oil from the Persian Gulf.

Western Front: British airmen bomb the Zeppelin factory at Friedrichshafen.

22

Eastern Front: In Galicia the Austrians lose heavily to the Russians on the Cracow-Chenstokhov front. 6,000 prisoners are taken.

Western Front: Trench warfare has become established all along the Western Front.

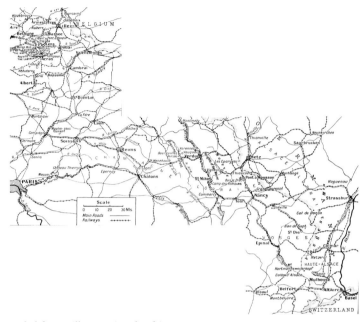

The French lines extended from Lille to Switzerland in 1915.

23

Eastern Front: In Poland the Russian line is broken by Mackensen south-east of Lodz.

Politics: The Portugese Congress agrees to side with the Allies.

War at sea: British squadron bombards Zeebrugge.
German submarine U-18 rammed by armed trawler Dorothy Gray , then sunk by HMS Garry in Pentland Firth.

Western Front: Ypres heavily bombed by the Germans, badly damaging the town and cathedral.

25

Western Front: Von Falkenhayn orders his troops to dig into defensive positions on high ground.
Arras suffers heavy German bombardment.

26

War at sea: Pre-dreadnought HMS Bulwark destroyed by ammo explosion in the Medway at Sheerness, 800 dead, only 12 survivors.

27

Western Front: Reims again heavily bombarded: President Wilson condemns such assaults on unfortified towns.

28

General: New York Stock Exchange reopens for bond trading for first time since July when it closed due to the war crisis.

29

Balkans: Start of the evacuation of Belgrade as the Austrians close in.

Eastern Front: Lodz is bombarded by the Germans.

Europe
rushes to war
JUL

Battle of Frontiers
in west;
Tannenberg in east
AUG

Invasion of France
SEP

Race to the Sea
reaches the Channel
OCT

Trench warfare
in west;
Mesopotamian
Front opens
NOV

Trench warfare
in east: Champagne
Offensive in west
DEC

Picking up brass shell cases after a bombardment on the Mesopotamian Front.

German troops dragging their trench mortar into position to support an attack.

Western Front: In Argonne the French retake almost all lost territory.

30
Western Front: King George visits British troops.

December 1914
President Woodrow Wilson tries to organize a peace as he reassures Americans that they won't get involved in the war and will remain strictly neutral.

1
Caucasus: Russians capture Sarai and Bashkal.

Eastern Front: Suburbs of Lodz see heavy fighting.

Western Front: King George visits Indian

The Kaiser decorates a soldier with the Iron Cross.

troops on the Western Front.
French troops recover Vermelles.

2
Balkans: Belgrade succumbs to Austrian occupation.

3
Balkans: Start of the Battle of the Ridges at Rudnik Malyen in Serbia.

5
Balkans: Battle of the Ridges ends when the Austrians are defeated: 15,000 prisoners taken.

Western Front: French airmen bomb German air sheds at Freiburg-in-Breisgau.

6
Politics: The Pope attempts to broker a Christmas truce.

39

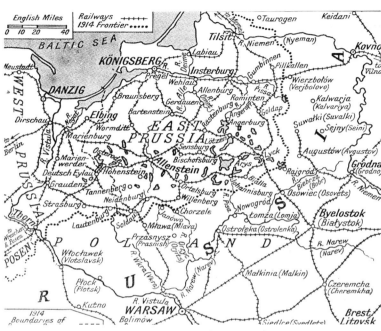

The Germans and Russians fought over East Prussia during the winter of 1914-15.

Eastern Front: Russians evacuate Lodz.

Western Front: Dunkirk undergoes long-distance German bombardment.

7

General: The French Bourse reopens.

Eastern Front: Second Battle for Warsaw.

Western Front: Egyptian Sirhind Brigade arrive at Western Front to complete the Indian Expeditionary Force.

8

Africa: In South Africa the rebellion collapses when 1,200 rebels surrender.

War at sea: In the Battle of the Falkland Islands Rear Admiral Sturdee's squadron sinks three German cruisers last encountered at the Battle of Coronel, only the Dresden escapes.

10

Politics: French government returns to Paris.

Eastern Front: 4,000 prisoners are taken when the Austrians are defeated near Cracow.

War at sea: Shipping around Dover is attacked by German submarines. Sturdee's squadron sinks Nürnberg.

Western Front: Germans again attack Ypres.

11

War at sea: The Goeben bombards Batoum.

13

Balkans: In Serbia the Austrians are completely routed.

War at sea: In the Dardanelles the Turkish battleship Messudiya is sunk by British submarine B.11.

Europe rushes to war
JUL

Battle of Frontiers in west; Tannenberg in east
AUG

Invasion of France
SEP

Race to the Sea reaches the Channel
OCT

Trench warfare in west; Mesopotamian Front opens
NOV

Trench warfare in east; Champagne Offensive in west
DEC

Top: General von Falkenhayn (wearing the cloak) was director of operations on the Western Front from December 1914 to August 1916.

King George V issuing decorations in the field, Flanders, end 1914.

Western Front: Germans withdraw from Yser Canal positions.

14

Western Front: Ypres attacked again by the Germans.

15

Balkans: In Serbia the Austrians evacuate Belgrade so ending their third invasion. Lost at least 28,000 prisoners and 70 guns.

War at sea: British fleet bombard Westeinde. In Syria HMS Doris bombards Alexandretta.

16

War at sea: The German First High Seas Fleet under Admiral Franz von Hipper bombard Hartlepool, Whitby, and Scarborough killing

German sentry standing guard outside a well sandbagged battalion HQ.

137 civilians and wounding 592. British coastal defense batteries damage three ships including the heavy cruiser Blucher. The Germans also lay offensive mines.

17

Eastern Front: In Poland the Germans occupy Petrokov.

Far East: The British proclaim Egypt as a British Protectorate.

Western Front: Armentières bombarded by the Germans.

18

Far East: Hussein I is proclaimed Sultan of Egypt.

War at sea: In the Baltic the German cruiser Friedrich Karl is reported lost.

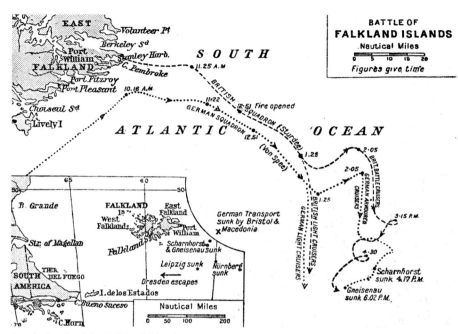

Map showing the battle of the Falkland Islands.

Western Front: Start of the Battle of Givenchy when Indian troops attack the German positions.

19

Africa: In South Africa the two remaining rebel leaders are condemned for treason. One is shot the other reprieved.

Western Front: German air sheds in Brussels are bombed by Allied airmen.

20

Western Front: Start of the First Battle of Champagne – the first major Allied offensive on the Western Front after the lines of trenches have been dug.

21

Western Front: BEF soldiers arrive to reinforce the Indian troops defending Givenchy. Together they hold the position

against severe opposition.
First German night bombing raid on Britain by a Farman MF-11.

23

Eastern Front: Siege of Cracow is abandoned by the Russians.

Far East: Troops from New Zealand and Australia arrive in Cairo.

Western Front: Belgian troops cross the Yser.

24

Africa: In South-West Africa German troops invade the Portuguese colony of Angola.

Eastern Front: Russia claims to have captured 134,000 German and 225,000 Austrians.

Western Front: A German FF29 seaplane makes the first air raid on Britain but drops

Europe
rushes to war
JUL

Battle of Frontiers
in west;
Tannenberg in east
AUG

Invasion of France
SEP

Race to the Sea
reaches the Channel
OCT

Trench warfare
in west;
Mespotamian
Front opens
NOV

Trench warfare
in east; Champagne
Offensive in west
DEC

Map of the Dardanelles and Gallipoli.
Bottom: Canadians carry wire to the front lines.

the bombs in the water off Dover.

Admiral Franz von Hipper led the German naval raid on Scarborough in December 1914.

25

Caucasus: In Armenia the Battle of Sarikamish starts as the Turks counter invade.

Eastern Front: The Austro-German offensive ends as they are defeated at Tarnow.

War at sea: British navy pilots supported by HMSs Arethusa and Undaunted bomb German warships off Cuxhaven.

Western Front: Unofficial Christmas truces spontaneously develop between rival soldiers along the Western Front. German FF29 returns to Britain and drops two bombs near Cliffe railway station, Kent.

26

Caucasus: In Armenia Turkish forces try to recapture Sarikamish in the Caucasus.

Eastern Front: Germans divert from attacking Warsaw to attack across Bzura.

Western Front: At Frescati near Metz French pilots bomb the German airsheds.

28

Caucasus: The Turks begin a disastrous retreat from Sarikamish. Many die of exposure in the mountains.

War at sea: In the North Sea freely drifting German mines destroy eight vessels.

30

Western Front: German planes attack Dunkirk.

31

General: The year ends with an estimated 753,000 Prussian losses.

1915

First use of gas
(on Eastern Front
in Poland)
JAN

Palestine
and Gallipoli
Fronts open
FEB

Russian offensive in
east; BEF attacks at
Neuve Chappelle
in west
MAR

Gallipoli landings;
Germans use gas
at Ypres
APR

Sinking of Lusitania;
first zeppelin raid
on London
MAY

Italian Front
opens

French troops receive decorations.

1915

January 1915

On the Western Front both sides launch repeated assaults in an attempt to break the deadlock. Russian troops active in Galicia.

1

General: Russia requests that Britain and France mount an attack on Turkey to relieve pressure on its southern flank.

War at sea: HMS Formidable torpedoed in the English Channel.

Western Front: Allied offensive in Artois and Champagne.

2

Africa: In German East Africa HMSs Fox and Goliath bombard German-held Dar-es-Salaam.

3

Eastern Front: Russians occupy Suczava.

4

Caucasus: Russians beat the Turks at Sarikamish in Russian Armenia and Ardahan in Transcaucasia.

Western Front: After several days fighting French troops take Steinbach in Alsace.

5

Western Front: In the Argonne the French blow up half a mile of German trenches.

8

Eastern Front/Balkans: Germany forms a southern army to support the faltering Austrians.

9

Africa: Last South African rebels are caught.

ussia retreats from Poland; Germany surrenders in SW Africa
JUL

Germans occupy Warsaw
AUG

Champagne and Artois-Loos offensives in west
SEP

Allies land in Salonika; Serbia invaded
OCT

Sebia collapses; British held in Mesopotamia at Ctesiphon
NOV

Siege of Kut; Haig becomes BEF commander
DEC

German U-boat demands the surrender of a British merchantman.

Bottom: German field artillery in Champagne.

Western Front: German counter-attacks at Perthes and near Soissons fail in the face of stiff Allied resistance.

12

Western Front: The Germans are reported to have fired poison shells.

13

Africa: In East Africa Germans attack the British at Jasin.

Caucasus: Battle of Kara Urgan in Armenia.

Eastern Front: Germans take the heights of Vregny.

14

Africa: South African Union forces occupy Swakopmund, in German South-West Africa.

The chalky soil of Champagne shows the zigzags of a French trench.

Western Front: ermans claim to have taken 5,200 prisoners as they win the fight near Soissons.

15

Far East: Japan makes 21 demands on China.

16

Caucasus: In Armenia the Russians rout the Turks following the Battle of Kara Urgan. They take 4.000 prisoners.

Eastern Front: Russians move along the Lower Vistula despite heavy resistance near Bolimov.

Western Front: French artillery blasts Germans out of their trenches at Nieuport.

17

War at sea: In the Dardanelles the French submarine Saphir is sunk.

First use of gas (on Eastern Front in Poland)
JAN

Palestine and Gallipoli Fronts open
FEB

Russian offensive in east; BEF attacks at Neuve Chappelle in west
MAR

Gallipoli landings; Germans use gas at Ypres
APR

Sinking of Lusitania; first zeppelin raid on London
MAY

Italian Front opens
J

Map of German East Africa.

19

Great Britain: Zeppelins belonging to the Imperial German Navy Airship Division make the first airship attack on Britain when they drop bombs on Great Yarmouth and King's Lynn, Norfolk. Five people are killed. The Royal Flying Corps flew its first night sorties to intercept the Zeppelins but failed to make contact.

21

War at sea: A German submarine sinks the British SS Durward near the Maas lightship. German submarine U-7 torpedoed off the Dutch coast in error by U-22. Only one survivor.

22

Eastern Front: Austrians prevail and win their attack on the Kirlibaba Pass (East Carpathians).

Western Front: Heavy fighting continues on the Western Front, especially in the Argonne and in Alsace.

24

War at sea: Battle of Dogger Bank starts when Germans attack the Dogger Bank patrols protecting the fishing fleet. The raid is intercepted and the heavy cruiser Blücher is sunk, battlecruisers Seydlitz and Derfflinger hit and damaged. British battlecruisers Lion (Vice-Admiral Beatty's flagship) damaged, Tiger hit. Both sides claimed the encounter as a victory.

25

Eastern Front: Libau forts shoot down a Zeppelin.
Hard fighting in the Carpathians between Russians and Austrians.

Russia retreats from Poland; Germany surrenders in SW Africa **JUL**

Germans occupy Warsaw **AUG**

Champagne and Artois-Loos offensives in west **SEP**

Allies land in Salonika; Serbia invaded **OCT**

Sebia collapses; British held in Mesopotamia at Ctesiphon **NOV**

Siege of Kut; Haig becomes BEF commander **DEC**

Top: Cheerful German soldiers march across the empty promenade at Ostend which in normal times would be thronging with holiday-makers.

Bottom: Exhausted British soldiers grab some rest from the stresses of the front line in temporary shelters.

Albert, King of the Belgians.

26
Caucasus: Turkey attacks again in Armenia.

War at sea: British announce the loss of HMS Viknor.

27
Western Front: In the Argonne the Allies prevail against German attacks.

28
Eastern Front: Trebizond and Rize bombarded by a Russian torpedo boat.

Western Front: Night raid on Dunkirk by a German plane.

29
Africa: Cameroons the French take Bertua.

War at sea: Skirmish off Cape Moen, Denmark: Russian submarine sinks a German torpedo boat.

Western Front: Germans fail to cross the Aisne near Soissons.

30
Eastern Front: At Sufian the Russians beat the Turks and drive them from Tabriz.

War at sea: Four British merchant ships are sunk off the Lancashire coast by German submarine activity.

Western Front: French suffer a reverse in the western Argonne and lose 700 men taken as prisoners.

February 1915
British casualties by this point of the war are estimated to be around 104,000. New fighting

1915

First use of gas (on Eastern Front in Poland) **JAN**

Palestine and Gallipoli Fronts open **FEB**

Russian offensive in east; BEF attacks at Neuve Chappelle in west **MAR**

Gallipoli landings; Germans use gas at Ypres **APR**

Sinking of Lusitania; first zeppelin raid on London **MAY**

Italian Front opens J

Battle of the Dogger Bank, January 24, 1915. Blücher moments before she sank.

fronts open in Palestine and Gallipoli. The latter became notorious for the heavy loss of ANZAC (from Australia and New Zealand) troops. Gallipoli itself is a narrow peninsula on the northwestern side of the Canakkale straits that link the Aegean Sea with the Sea of Marmara.

1

Eastern Front: The Russians gain the initiative and make ground.

General: Flour and bread are rationed in Germany.

Middle East: Turks start to advance in strength (c. 12,000 men) towards the Suez Canal.

War at sea: German submarine attacks Asturias, a hospital ship, off Le Havre.

2

Middle East: Defense of the Suez Canal. Indian troops supported by Egyptian artillery repulse attacking Turks at the Suez Canal.

4

War at sea: Announcement of unrestricted submarine warfare in British waters by Germany with a submarine blockade as of 18 February. Neutral ships enter at their own risk.

6

Eastern Front: Second Battle of Masurian Lakes – aka the Winter Battle – the German armies are surrounded by the Russians.

War at sea: The American liner Lusitania docks at Liverpool.

7

Eastern Front: The Germans advance 25 miles despite heavy fighting.

ussia retreats from Poland; Germany Surrenders in SW Africa **JUL**

Germans occupy Warsaw **AUG**

Champagne and Artois-Loos offensives in west **SEP**

Allies land in Salonika; Serbia invaded **OCT**

Sebia collapses; British held in Mesopotamia at Ctesiphon **NOV**

Siege of Kut; Haig becomes BEF commander **DEC**

Zeppelin leaving its hangar in front of an enormous crowd.

Bottom: Two German destroyers at quayside in Zeebrugge being loaded with mines before sailing to the North Sea where they will rendezvous and resupply submarines and mine layers.

Western Front: In the Argonne Germans launch a heavy assault at Bagatelle.

8
Far East: Turks in full retreat from the Suez Canal.

War at sea: In the Crimea the Breslau bombs Yalta.
Trebizond is bombarded by Russian cruisers.

11
Western Front: First Canadian soldiers land in France.

12
Eastern Front: Germans continue to make good progress in Poland and east Prussia.

Reims, despite being severely damaged by German bombing was never taken by the enemy.

Western Front: Ostend, Zeebrugge and other German-held Belgian ports are raided by 34 British naval planes.

13
Eastern Front: Fierce fighting in the Carpathians.

Middle East: A surprise attack by the British at Tor on the Gulf of Suez leave 60 Turks dead and 102 taken prisoner.

14
Eastern Front: The Russians are completely driven out of East Prussia.

Western Front: Wins and losses for all sides on the Western Front as the battles fluctuate.

15
Balkans: Albanians are reported to have advanced into Serbia.

First use of gas (on Eastern Front in Poland)
JAN

Palestine and Gallipoli Fronts open
FEB

Russian offensive in east; BEF attacks at Neuve Chappelle in west
MAR

Gallipoli landings; Germans use gas at Ypres
APR

Sinking of Lusitania; first zeppelin raid on London
MAY

Italian Front opens
J

French troops in early 1915.

16

Western Front: Fighting heavy in the Argonne and Champagne region.
More Allied air raids on German-held Belgian ports.

17

Eastern Front: Heavy fighting at Kolomea on the River Pruth and Nadworna.

18

War at sea: German submarine blockade around the British Isles. They declare the waters around Great Britain and Ireland to be a 'war region' – meaning all vessels of any nation are a viable target.

Western Front: Main fighting on the Western Front at Verdun, Arras and in Alsace.

19

Eastern Front: Russians start a counter-offensive on the East Prussian frontier.

War at sea: In the English Channel the Norwegian SS Belridge is torpedoed, but not sunk.
At the entrance of the Dardanelles three French and five British warships start to bombard the Turkish forts in preparation for an attack on Constantinople.

Western Front: Heavy fighting in the Vosges.

21

Eastern Front: End of the Second Battle of the Masurian Lakes with the Russians taking heavy losses. Elsewhere on the Eastern Front they make some gains.

Great Britain: German planes bomb Colchester, Essex and area.

Russia retreats from Poland, Germany surrenders in SW Africa
JUL

Germans occupy Warsaw
AUG

Champagne and Artois-Loos offensives in west
SEP

Allies land in Salonika; Serbia invaded
OCT

Serbia collapses; British held in Mesopotamia at Ctesiphon
NOV

Siege of Kut; Haig becomes BEF commander
DEC

Australian troops in front of the Sphinx.
Bottom: Australian troops, Egypt, 1915.

The Eastern Front from Kovno in the north to the frontiers of Romania — showing the area over which the Russians made a fighting retreat in 1915. Inset: district around the Gulf of Riga.

22

Eastern Front: Intensive fighting, start of the battle around Dalina-Stanislau. Germans announce complete victory in East Prussia, claim 100,000 Russian prisoners.

Western Front: Calais is bombed by Zeppelins. Reims is heavily bombed again.

23

War at sea: German submarine sinks the U.S. ships Carib and Evelyn and torpedoes the Norwegian ship Regin.

24

Eastern Front: The Germans take Przasnysz with 10,000 prisoners. Meanwhile the Russians take Mozelny.

War at sea: British admit loss of auxillary cruiser Clan McNaughton.
Allied bombardment continues on Dardanelles

forts destroying some of the outer forts.
After a week of the submarine blockade seven British merchant ships have been sunk.

26

War at sea: The entrance to the Dardanelles is cleared of Turkish defense.

27

Eastern Front: Russians retake Przasnysz, report 5,400 prisoners.

War at sea: Admiralty announces a blockade of East African ports.
First U.S. shipping loss. The William P. Frye taking wheat to England is stopped by a German cruiser and ordered to jettison her cargo. William P. Frye judged not to have complied is sunk in the South Atlantic off the Brazilian coast.

First use of gas (on Eastern Front in Poland) **JAN**

Palestine and Gallipoli Fronts open **FEB**

Russian offensive in east; BEF attacks at Neuve Chappelle in west **MAR**

Gallipoli landings; Germans use gas at Ypres **APR**

Sinking of Lusitania; first zeppelin raid on London **MAY**

Italian Front opens J

German machine gunners in Poland, 1915.

28
General: U.S. Congress creates the United States Coast Guard.

31
Eastern Front: Start of the Battle of Bolimov in Poland. Poison gas is used for the first time: Germans use xylyl bromide against Russian soldiers at Bolimov.

March 1915
Fierce fighting in the Dardanelles. All the main battle fronts are reinforced with manpower and guns.

1
Eastern Front: German offensive collapses along the Niemen River.

War at sea: British passenger liner Falaba sinks, claiming the first American casualty of the war.

2
Eastern Front: Russians reported to have taken over 10,000 German prisoners from the Niemen River front fighting.

Middle East: Allied troops land at Kum-Kale, on the Asiatic side of the Dardanelles.

3
Eastern Front: Austrians involved in fierce fighting in the Carpathians.

Western Front: Reims bombarded again.

4
Eastern Front: After taking Stanislau and Krasna the Russians claim to have taken 19,000 German prisoners.

War at sea: In the English Channel German submarine U8 is sunk by destroyers and the crew rescued.

Russia retreats from Poland; Germany surrenders in SW Africa **JUL**

Germans occupy Warsaw **AUG**

Champagne and Artois-Loos offensives in west **SEP**

Allies land in Salonika; Serbia invaded **OCT**

Serbia collapses; British held in Mesopotamia at Ctesiphon **NOV**

Siege of Kut; Haig becomes BEF commander **DEC**

German prisoners hauling a machine-gun out of a captured dug-out in Arras.

German submarine rammed and sunk by SS Thordis.

5

Middle East: Forts in the Dardanelles narrows bombarded by HMS Queen Elizabeth.

Western Front: German Zepplin destroyed near Tirlemont.

6

Eastern Front: Austrians retreating in the Carpathians.

7

Eastern Front: In north Poland the Germans retreat through Augustovo Woods from pursuing Russian forces.

Western Front: Six British aviators bomb Ostend.

8

Eastern Front: Fierce fighting north of the Vistula — gains and losses for both sides.

Middle East: Bombardments on Dardanelles forts are halted by bad weather.

War at sea: Russian Black Sea Fleet bombards Turkish coastal positions.

10

War at sea: HMSs Ariel and Attack ram and sink submarine U-12 in Fife Ness. Ten survivors are captured.

Western Front: Start of the Battle of Neuve-Chapelle when the BEF attack German lines. RFC makes its first bomb raids against enemy railroad installations. Also the first attack planned with the use of maps drawn only from aerial photo reconnaissance.

1915

First use of gas (on Eastern Front in Poland)
JAN

Palestine and Gallipoli Fronts open
FEB

Russian offensive in east; BEF attacks at Neuve Chappelle in west
MAR

Gallipoli landings; Germans use gas at Ypres
APR

Sinking of Lusitania; first zeppelin raid on London
MAY

Italian Front opens
JU

After resting in billets, men from the Loyal North Lancashire Regiment make their way back to the front.

11

Eastern Front: Germans start new offensive near Przasnysz.

Great Britain: Britain announces blockade of German ports and issues the Reprisals Order banning 'neutral' parties trading with Germany.

War at sea: Off Scottish coast British auxiliary cruiser Bayona torpedoed and sunk.

13

Western Front: Ypres suffers bombardments again.

14

War at sea: Off Juan Fernandez in Chilean territorial waters British warships Kent, Orama, and Glasgow sink the German battleship Dresden.

Western Front: Start of the Battle of St. Eloi as the Germans attack Ypres.

16

Western Front: French forces make good progress in Champagne, Argonne and to the north of Mesnil.

18

Eastern Front: Austrians still attacking without progress in the Carpathians. .

Middle East: Allied plan to invade the Dardanelles is drawn up following the failed naval attempt to force the Narrows in the Battle of Canakkale in which the Turkish fleet was victorious. HMSs Ocean and Irresistible and French warship Bouvet are sunk.

19

Western Front: Germans launch a heavy assault in the Vosges.

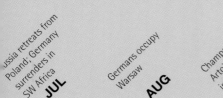
Russia retreats from Poland; Germany surrenders in SW Africa **JUL**

Germans occupy Warsaw **AUG**

Champagne and Artois-Loos offensives in west **SEP**

Allies land in Salonika; Serbia invaded **OCT**

Serbia collapses; British held in Mesopotamia at Ctesiphon **NOV**

Siege of Kut; Haig becomes BEF commander **DEC**

Two Germans take cover as a third throws a stick grenade.

Clouds of German poison gas drift towards Russian lines.

20

Middle East/War at sea: Violent storms in the Dardanelles halt hostilities.

22

Eastern Front: Austrian fortress of Przemysl surrenders to the Russians – siege started 11 November 1914 – taking 126,000 Austro-Hungarian prisoners.

Western Front: Two Zeppelins attack Paris.

23

Middle East: Near El Kubri British soldiers rout raiding Turkish forces.

Western Front: German guns bombard Reims and Soissons.

24

Politics: Chile makes a diplomatic protest to Britain about violation of her territorial

waters during the battle off Juan Fernandez (14 March).

Western Front: British naval airmen raid Hoboken near Antwerp.

25

Eastern Front: Russian counter offensive in the Carpathians: take 5,700 prisoners.

War at sea: First neutral ship to be sunk after a stop and search. German submarine U-29 captures and sinks Dutch SS Medea.

26

Western Front: Six French airmen bomb Metz.

28

War at sea: SS Falaba outbound for South Africa sunk by German torpedoes. 100 lives lost, many of them women and children.

1915

First use of gas
(on Eastern Front
in Poland)
JAN

Palestine
and Gallipoli
Fronts open
FEB

Russian offensive in
east; BEF attacks at
Neuve Chappelle
in west **MAR**

Gallipoli landings;
Germans use gas
at Ypres
APR

Sinking of Lusitania;
first zeppelin raid
on London
MAY

Italian Front
opens
JU

Wayside dressing station as the wounded are brought in after an attack. Lightly wounded made their own way, those needing more attention visited first aid posts before walking to the dressing station, while severely wounded arrived on stretchers.

Russian Black Sea Fleet bombards Bosphorus forts.

April 1915

Reports start to reach the Allies of the Turkish massacre of some 800,000 Armenians. Germans attention is primarily on the Eastern Front where they attempt to break through Gorlice-Tarnow and force Russia out of Poland. Italy renounces the Central Powers and joins the Allies.

1

Africa: In German South-West Africa South African troops occupy Hasuur.

War at sea: British SS Seven Seas torpedoed off Beachy Head.

Western Front: British air raid on Zeebrugge and Hoboken.

2

Eastern Front: Russian cavalry defeat the German cavalry in north Poland.

War at sea: In the North Sea German submarine U-10 sinks British trawlers Nellie, Gloxinia, and Jason.

3

Middle East: French expeditionary force starts to disembark at Alexandria.

War at sea: Russian Black Sea Fleet engage Goeben and Breslau.
Off Odessa Turkish cruiser Medjidia is sunk by a mine.

4

Caucasus: In Armenia the Russian beat the Turks at Olty.

Russia retreats from Poland; Germany surrenders in SW Africa **JUL**

Germans occupy Warsaw **AUG**

Champagne and Artois-Loos offensives in west **SEP**

Allies land in Salonika; Serbia invaded **OCT**

Sebia collapses; British held in Mesopotamia at Ctesiphon **NOV**

Siege of Kut; Haig becomes BEF commander **DEC**

The air war intensified throughout the conflict.

German troops rest up during the day in preparation for a night raiding party.

Eastern Front: Germans bomb a Russian hospital at Radom, Poland.

8

Caucasus: The Ottoman Empire begins a program of deportation and massacre against the Armenians starting in Cilicia.

9

Gallipoli: Near the Dardenelles British and French forces led by Generals Hamilton and d'Amade start to gather.

Western Front: French troops capture Les Eparges.

10

Balkans: Belgrade is shelled by an Austrian gunboat.

Politics: Germany protests to the U.S. about her pro-Allied stance.

War at sea: While engaged in Belgian relief work and holding a German safe conduct pass British steamer Harpalyce is torpedoed without warning by UB-4, midway between Harwich and the Hook of Holland. 15 crewmen lost.

11

Mesopotamia: British troops attacked by Turks at Kurna and in the Persian Gulf at Ahwaz.

War at sea: Harrison liner Wayfarer torpedoed.

12

Middle East: Gaza bombarded by French cruiser St. Louis.

Western Front: German airship bombs Nancy.

1915

First use of gas
(on Eastern Front
in Poland) **JAN**

Palestine
and Gallipoli
Fronts open **FEB**

Russian offensive in
east; BEF attacks at
Neuve Chappelle
in west **MAR**

Gallipoli landings;
Germans use gas
at Ypres **APR**

Sinking of Lusitania;
first zeppelin raid
on London **MAY**

Italian Front
opens J

Carpathians, 1915. The Austrians retreat from the Russian advance leaving their dead and munitions as they go.

14

Great Britain: German Zeppelins raid Tyneside.

Politics: Australian government confirms that it will send every available man to support the Allies in the war.

15

War at sea: Russian Black Sea Fleet bombs Anatolian coastal positions.

Western Front: 15 Allied planes bomb Ostend. Freiburg bombed by French airship.

16

Great Britain: German Zeppelins raid East Anglia, England. .
Faversham and Sittingbourne in Kent are bombed by German planes.

War at sea: El Arish bombarded by French cruiser. Turkish torpedo boat sinks British transport Manitou. 51 lives are lost.

22

War at sea: Due to shipping losses British Admiralty suspends passenger traffic between Britain and the Netherlands.

Western Front: Second Battle of Ypres sees first use of poison gas on the Western Front. German Fourth Army launces a surprise attack on Canadian troops at Ypres. However, the Canadians manage to check the German advance.
German use chlorine gas against British forces at Langemarck.

23

Italian Front: Italy declares war on Austria-Hungary and begins invasion on a 60-mile front. creating another battle front.

Russia retreats from Poland; Germany surrenders in SW Africa
JUL

Germans occupy Warsaw
AUG

Champagne and Artois-Loos offensives in west
SEP

Allies land in Salonika; Serbia invaded
OCT

Serbia collapses; British held in Mesopotamia at Ctesiphon
NOV

Siege of Kut; Haig becomes BEF commander
DEC

In the sky over Paris a light French plane swoops to do battle with a slow-moving German Zeppelin.

Bottom: German machine gun post ready to cover a new attack.

Politics: Britain declares a blockade of the Cameroons.

War at sea: Allied fleet bombard Turkish coast in the Gulf of Saros.

24

Africa: In German East Africa there is fighting around Mount Kilimanjaro.

25

Gallipoli: 70,000 British and French troops land at at Helles & Anzac Cove, Gallipoli to try to take Turkey out of the war. Immediate heavy fighting.

War at sea: Russian Black Sea Fleet shells forts around the Bosphorus coast.

View of Scapa Flow, the great British Navy base in the Orkneys. It was large enough to easily accommodate the entire Grand Fleet.

26

Politics: Italy joins the Entente on signing the secret Treaty of London with Britain, France, and Russia.

War at sea: Under international law the armed German liner Kronprinz Wilhelm is interned at Newport News, VA. after being forced into port. She had sunk over 60,000 tons of Allied shipping.

27

Gallipoli: The Allies are established across the peninsula.

Western Front: Germans again deploy gas during the Second Battle of Ypres.

28

Eastern Front: Germans and Austrians led by von Mackensen mount a strong new offensive which drives the Russians back.

1915

First use of gas (on Eastern Front in Poland) **JAN**

Palestine and Gallipoli Fronts open **FEB**

Russian offensive in east; BEF attacks at Neuve Chappelle in west **MAR**

Gallipoli landings; Germans use gas at Ypres **APR**

Sinking of Lusitania; first zeppelin raid on London **MAY**

Italian Front opens

Russian troops surrendering — they would be put to work as captive labour in munition factories or on the land.

Gallipoli: supported by Queen Elizabeth, Allies advance to First Battle of Krithia and of Krithia when the.

29

Middle East: Turks withdraw from the Suez Canal region.

War at sea: In the Sea of Marmora submarine E14 sinks a Turkish transport.

Western Front: Canadian troops are withdrawn from Ypres.

30

General: Germany publishes a newspaper warning to U.S. citizens not to sail in the Lusitania.

War at sea: In the Sea of Marmora a Turkish warship sinks Australian submarine AE2.

Great Britain: Zeppelins again raid East Anglia.

31

Great Britain: German Zeppelins bombard the London suburbs.

May 1915

The Russian armies in Poland collapse. The sinking of the liner Lusitania provokes an international outrage and horror and a German-American crisis when a large number of Americans lose their lives. In Gallipoli the Allied ANZAC soldiers are unable to break out of the peninsula.

1

Far East: Chinese demand the restoration of Kiao-chau from Japan.
Gallipoli: Fierce fighting between Turkish and Allied forces as Turks counter attack at Eski

Russia retreats from Poland; Germany surrenders in SW Africa **JUL**

Germans occupy Warsaw **AUG**

Champagne and Artois-Loos offensives in west **SEP**

Allies land in Salonika; Serbia invaded **OCT**

Sebia collapses; British held in Mesopotamia at Ctesiphon **NOV**

Siege of Kut; Haig becomes BEF commander **DEC**

British troops trundling wire hoops through the mud up to the front lines.

Improvised Lewis gun table. The gun is tied by a cord to a wheel revolving on a pole securely fixed in the ground.

Hissarlik.

War at sea: First U.S. ship attacked by German submarines: oil tanker Gulflight torpedoed off the Scilly Isles by German submarine U-30, she was badly damaged but did not sink: three lives lost.

2

Africa: In German Southwest Africa British South Africa troops under General Botha capture Otymbingue,.

Eastern Front: Start of major Austro-German offensive in Galicia at Gorlice-Tarnow. By summer's end Germany controls an area covered by present-day Poland, Lithuania, Belarus and Ukraine.

War at sea: Russian Black Sea Fleet shells Bosphorus forts.

Troops of the London Rifle Brigade 'taking it easy' in a reserve trench.

3

Politics: Italy denounces the Triple Alliance, in particular Austrian actions in July 1914.

4

Western Front: A kite balloon is used for artillery observation for the first time.

6

Gallipoli: Second Battle of Krithia begins.

7

Eastern Front: Germans capture the Russian Baltic port of Libau.

General: Christians are massacred in the Ottoman Empire.

1915

First use of gas (on Eastern Front in Poland)
JAN

Palestine and Gallipoli Fronts open
FEB

Russian offensive in east; BEF attacks at Neuve Chappelle in west
MAR

Gallipoli landings; Germans use gas at Ypres
APR

Sinking of Lusitania; first zeppelin raid on London
MAY

Italian Front opens
J

River Clyde, a 4,000-ton collier, played a significant part in the April 25, 1915 landings. She was run ashore on V beach with 2,000 troops on board.

War at sea: British Cunard liner Lusitania en route from New York to Liverpool torpedoed without warning and sunk within 18 minutes by German submarine U-20 off the Irish coast at Kinsale Head. 1,195 lives (out of 1,959) are lost, including 124 American passengers.

9

Western Front: Battle of Aubers Ridge – a British preliminary bombardment – starts the Artois Offensive. The main battle was a French attempt to break through the Germans lines with a massive infantry assault.

13

Eastern Front: End of the Battle of Gorlice-Tarnow, in which the Germans push the Russians into retreat.

War at sea: In the Dardanelles HMS Goliath is struck by three Turkish torpedos from Muavenet. 570 sailors are lost.

Western Front: Heavy German bombardments at Ypres.

14

Eastern Front: Russians take Kolomea and Austro-Germans take Jaroslav.

Politics: Britain begins to intern enemy aliens.

Western Front: End of the Second battle of Ypres leaves the town largely as rubble. BEF casualties are triple those of Germans.

15

Western Front: Battle of Festubert in the Ypres salient starts with British attack. During the battle British, Indian, and Canadian troops are involved.

Russia retreats from Poland; Germany surrenders in SW Africa **JUL**

Germans occupy Warsaw **AUG**

Champagne and Artois-Loos offensives in west **SEP**

Allies land in Salonika; Serbia invaded **OCT**

Sebia collapses; British held in Mesopotamia at Ctesiphon **NOV**

Siege of Kut; Haig becomes BEF commander **DEC**

Map of Gallipoli peninsula showing British, Australian and New Zealand landing points in April 1915. The inset shows Cape Hellesand the five British landing beaches.

Australian troops, Anzac Cove, land a field gun.

17
Great Britain: Zeppelins raid Dunkirk and Ramsgate.

19
Gallipoli: Start of the Turkish attack at Anzac Cove.

20
Eastern Front: Przemysl bombarded by von Mackensen's troops.

22
Politics: Italy orders the mobilization of her troops.

War at sea: In the Black Sea the Russian battleship Penteleimon is torpedoed.

Western Front: Paris undergoes German air raid.

French gunners, Gallipoli.

63

First use of gas (on Eastern Front in Poland) **JAN**

Palestine and Gallipoli Fronts open **FEB**

Russian offensive in east; BEF attacks at Neuve Chappelle in west **MAR**

Gallipoli landings; Germans use gas at Ypres **APR**

Sinking of Lusitania; first zeppelin raid on London **MAY**

Italian Front opens

THE DAILY TELEGRAPH, SATURDAY MAY 8, 1915.

LUSITANIA TORPEDOED : 1,400 LIVES LOST

The Daily Telegraph records the sinking of the Lusitania, May 7, 1915.

23

Italian Front: On the Southern Front Austrian troops attack in the Carnic Alps.

Politics: Despite treaty agreements with the Central Powers, Italy declares war on Austria-Hungary.

24

Italian Front: On the Isonzo Front Italian troops occupy Caporetto and Cormons; and advance towards Trentino and Carnic.

War at sea: Austrian naval raids along the Italian Adriatic coast and first air raid over Venice.

Western Front: The Allies make headway on the Western Front.

25

General: Turkey expelles Christian Armenians from their homeland to Aleppo in Syria: leads to deaths of some 800,000 men, women and children.

Italian Front: Italians capture Monte Altinino in Trentino.

Politics: Britain forms a coalition government when PM Asquith reorganizes his Liberal government as a coalition of the parties.

War at sea: Off Gallipoli HMS Triumph is torpedoed.
U.S. ship SS Nebraskan is torpedoed.

Western Front: End of the Battle of Festubert when Allies captured the village. Allies won less than half a mile of territory and lost some 16,000 men during the battle. Germany

Russia retreats from Poland; Germany surrenders in SW Africa **JUL**

Germans occupy Warsaw **AUG**

Champagne and Artois-Loos offensives in west **SEP**

Allies land in Salonika; Serbia invaded **OCT**

Sebia collapses; British held in Mesopotamia at Ctesiphon **NOV**

Siege of Kut; Haig becomes BEF commander **DEC**

Austrian troops flood into Prezemysl after retaking it in May 1915.

Bottom: British troops after gas attack.

Damage to Bartholomew Close, London, after a Zeppelin attack.

abandons Ypres offensive ending the Second Battle of Ypres: 105,000 Allied casualties.

26

Great Britain: Zeppelins raid Southend on the Essex coast of England.

27

War at sea: In Sheerness harbor British minelayer HMS Irene is blown up.
Off Gallipoli HMS Majestic is torpedoed.

31

Great Britain: First Zeppelin raid on London. LZ-38 kills seven people and injures 35. Damage estimated at some £19,000.

June 1915

The Italian Front opens up as Austria and

Italy fight for advantage in the first of the ten, eleven or even twelve battles of the Isonzo (experts disagree about which battles strictly count). Poland is increasingly occupied by Austro-German troops.

1

Eastern Front: Germans use gas in an attack west of Warsaw.

Italian Front: Bari and Brindisi bombed by Austrian planes.

Mesopotamia: Turks retreat along the Tigris pursued by British naval flotilla.

3

Eastern Front: After fierce fighting Austro-German troops retake Przemysl.

65

First use of gas (on Eastern Front in Poland) **JAN**

Palestine and Gallipoli Fronts open **FEB**

Russian offensive in east; BEF attacks at Neuve Chappelle in west **MAR**

Gallipoli landings; Germans use gas at Ypres **APR**

Sinking of Lusitania; first zeppelin raid on London **MAY**

Italian Front opens J

Italian troops dig in 10,000ft above sea level.

Western Front: british take the trenches at Givenchy.

4

Gallipoli: Start of the Third Battle of Krithia. Initially successful, it turns into a costly failure with the loss of 6,000 men.

6

Great Britain: Zeppelin raids on the east coast of England kill 24 and injure 30.

8

Western Front: French make important gains at Neuville St. Vaast, in 'The Labyrinth' (north of Arras) and at Hébuterne.

15

Western Front: Zeppelins raid the north-east coast of Britain.
Karlsruhe in Baden bombed by French airmen.

17

Italian Front: Italian troops capture the heights above the left bank of the Isonzo overlooking Plava.

Western Front: Retreating Germans torch Metzeral in Alsace.

18

War at sea: Austrian warships carry out raids along the Italian Adriatic.

22

Eastern Front: Lemberg (Lvov) is recaptured by the Austrians.

Italian Front: Italy starts the Isonzo Offensive (the first of 10, some count 12, attacks) against fortified Austrian positions along a 50-mile front in the Trentino area and central Isonzo around Gorizia.

Russia retreats from Poland; Germany surrenders in SW Africa **JUL**

Germans occupy Warsaw **AUG**

Champagne and Artois-Loos offensives in west **SEP**

Allies land in Salonika; Serbia invaded **OCT**

Serbia collapses; British held in Mesopotamia at Ctesiphon **NOV**

Siege of Kut; Haig becomes BEF commander **DEC**

Bersaglieri in a trench overlooking the River Eisack.

Bottom: The Minenwerfer or 'Minnie' was first used as shown here on the Isonzo front. Designed by the Krupp Works at Essen, it had a 2in calibre and fired a 250lb spherical bomb to a maximum range of 450 yards.

Western Front: Fierce fighting along the River Meuse with both sides winning and losing ground.

26
Balkans: Montenegrin soldiers enter Scutari in Albania.

Western Front: Start of the Battle of the Argonne.

27
Eastern Front: Russian setbacks on the Eastern Front see them retreating in Galicia.

Gallipoli: The Allies take four Turkish lines near Krithia.Positions on the Asia Minor coats are bombed by HMS Hussar.

Italian troops check a civilian: spies abounded in territories taken from the enemy.

28
War at sea: Windau in the Baltic is bombarded by German warships.

29
Eastern Front: Major Austro-German advance towards the rivers Vistula and Bug.

30
Italian Front: French forces take six lines of Turkish trenches.

July 1915
After taking heavy losses on the Eastern Front – especially in Poland – the Russian command decides to withdraw their troops from Poland.

First use of gas (on Eastern Front in Poland) **JAN**

Palestine and Gallipoli Fronts open **FEB**

Russian offensive in east; BEF attacks at Neuve Chappelle in west **MAR**

Gallipoli landings; Germans use gas at Ypres **APR**

Sinking of Lusitania; first zeppelin raid on London **MAY**

Italian Front opens **J**

Artillery is manhandled in the mountainous region between Austria and Italy as an Italian infantry battalion marches past.

1

War at sea: Off the Cornish coast of Britain Leyland liner Armenian is torpedoed.

2

Eastern Front: Austrians occupy Krasnik.

Italian Front: The great Battle for Carso Plateau begins.

War at sea: In Danzig Bay the German cruiser Pomern is sunk by a British submarine.
Off Gothland Russian warships sink the Albatross.
Off Yarmouth Germarine submarine UC2 unwittingly rammed by steamer Cottingham. Wreck investigators recovered her code book and papers.

3

Africa: In South Africa, General Smuts offers a contingent of volunteer soldiers to the Allies: gratefully accepted on 6 July.

Gallipoli: Since 29 June Turks have lost 5,150 soldiers killed and a further 15,000 taken prisoner.

4

War at sea: Off Cape Hellas French liner Carthage is torpedoed and sunk.
In German East Africa trapped (on Rufıji River) German cruiser Königsberg is disabled by monitors.

Western Front: Battle of the Argonne diminishes and ends.

5

Eastern Front: Austro-German troops attempt to move north from Galicia towards Kholm-Lyublin line is halted, following a heavy

JUL Russia retreats from Poland; Germany surrenders in SW Africa

AUG Germans occupy Warsaw

SEP Champagne and Artois-Loos offensives in west

OCT Allies land in Salonika; Serbia invaded

NOV Sebia collapses; British held in Mesopotamia at Ctesiphon

DEC Siege of Kut; Haig becomes BEF commander

Making bombs in early 1915, Gallipoli.

Top: Wounded on Gallipoli were exacuated to Mudros and Lemnos.

defeat between the rivers Vistula and Bug.

Western Front: Fierce fighting on the Meuse, around Arras and Souchez.

6

Eastern Front: Austrians beaten near Krasnik: Russians capture 15,000 prisoners in the surrounding countryside.

8

Africa: In German South-West Africa Union troops reach Tsumbeb and release all captured prisoners.

Italian Front: In Trentino the Italians take Monticello.

War at sea: In the Mediterranean the Italian cruiser Amalfi is sunk by an Austrian torpedo.

Bomb damage to London.

Western Front: French victory at Fontenelle in the Vosges.

9

Africa: German South-West Africa (now Namibia) surrenders unconditionally to British South African troops led by General Botha.

Italian Front: In Trentino Italians capture Costa Bella and Malga Sarta.

11

Africa: On the Rufiji River in German East Africa the Königsberg is finally destroyed.

Eastern Front: Heavy fighting on the Lyublin front sees Austrians losing ground.

Italian Front: Venice is bombed for the fourth time by Austrian planes.

1915

First use of gas (on Eastern Front in Poland) **JAN**

Palestine and Gallipoli Fronts open **FEB**

Russian offensive in east; BEF attacks at Neuve Chappelle in west **MAR**

Gallipoli landings; Germans use gas at Ypres **APR**

Sinking of Lusitania; first zeppelin raid on London **MAY**

Italian Front opens J

"Annie" at work, Gallipoli.

12

Africa: Skirmishes are reported between British-Belgian troops and Germans on the Northern Rhodesian frontier.

Eastern Front: Austro-German troops attack north east of Warsaw on the Bobr and Narev fronts.

Gallipoli: Turkish trenches in front of Achi Baba are captured.

13

Western Front: Germany starts a new offensive in the Argonne.

14

Eastern Front: Beginning of the massive Austro-German Triple Offensive from the Baltic to Bukovina. The Russians are forced to withdraw towards the Narev.

Western Front: A German attack on the Yser Canal is repulsed by Belgian soldiers.

15

Eastern Front: Russians forced into further retreats.

Western Front: Germans sustain heavy losses around the Yser.

16

Western Front: Renewed German attacks in Lorraine and west of Soissons.

17

Eastern Front: Desperate fighting between the rivers Vistula and Bug as the Austro-German forces advance.

Politics: A secret treaty is signed between Bulgaria and Turkish-German alliance.

Russia retreats from Poland; Germany surrenders in SW Africa
JUL

Germans occupy Warsaw
AUG

Champagne and Artois-Loos offensives in west
SEP

Allies land in Salonika; Serbia invaded
OCT

Serbia collapses; British held in Mesopotamia at Ctesiphon
NOV

Siege of Kut; Haig becomes BEF commander
DEC

British troops depart Boulogne for leave in Britain. The cross-Channel ferry used as a trooper is camouflaged in dazzle comouflage.

Italian troops creeping into the sap of a front line trench in preparation for a lightning raid on the Isonzo front.

18

Eastern Front: Russians retreating all along Vistula and Bug front and in full retreat north and west of Warsaw.

Italian Front: Start of the Second Battle of the Isonzo: Italians take 2,000 prisoners.

War at sea: Italian cruiser Guiseppe Garibaldi torpedoed.

19

Gallipoli: In London in the House of Commons Dardanelles Allied casualties to 30 June are announced as 42,434.

Western Front: Germans attack near Verdun and around Souchez.

20

Eastern Front: Fierce fighting especially south of Ivangorod, around the Bubissa, and during the Russian defense of the Lyublin-Kholm railroad.

21

Eastern Front: As Russian resistance collapses Germany starts to remove troops from the Eastern Front to the Western Front.

Mesopotamia: A British force reaches the River Euphrates and captures Turkish troops.

United States: President Wilson orders his Secretaries of War and the Navy to draft a defense program.

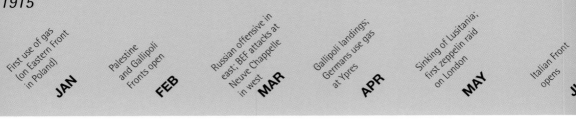

First use of gas (on Eastern Front in Poland) **JAN**

Palestine and Gallipoli Fronts open **FEB**

Russian offensive in east; BEF attacks at Neuve Chappelle in west **MAR**

Gallipoli landings; Germans use gas at Ypres **APR**

Sinking of Lusitania; first zeppelin raid on London **MAY**

Italian Front opens **JU**

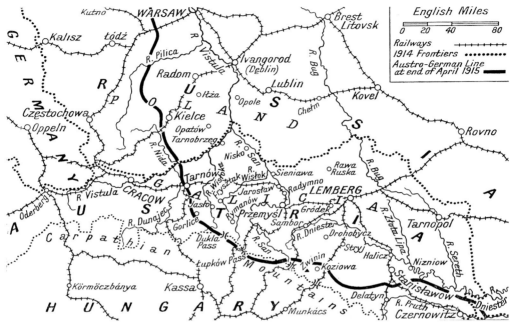

The great Austro-German campaigns that resulted in the conquest of much of Poland and the recovery of nearly all the province of Galicia, lost by Austria in 1914.

22

Eastern Front: Severe Russian losses force the leadership to announce the 'Great Retreat.' Russian troops are ordered out of Galicia taking their equipment and machinery with them.

Italian Front: Fierce fighting around the bridgehead of Gorizia sees Italian troops holding out against the Austrians.

23

Italian Front: Innsbruck is bombed.

Middle East: In Tripoli the Italian garrisons are massacred in the revolt of Senussites.

War at sea: In the Adriatic Austrian warships bombard Ortona and the Tremiti Islands.

24

United States: Public opinion is stirred up by strikes and rumors of German sabotage in U.S. munition factories.

25

Africa: In the Cameroons the French occupy Lomie.

Mesopotamia: Nasriya is bombarded, attacked, and occupied by British troops under General Gorringe.

War at sea: U.S. steamer Leelanaw is torpedoed.

Western Front: The first RFC fighter squadron – No 11 Sqn – arrives in France equipped with 2-seater Vickers FB5 Gunbus planes.

Russia retreats from Poland; Germany surrenders in SW Africa **JUL**

Germans occupy Warsaw **AUG**

Champagne and Artois-Loos offensives in west **SEP**

Allies land in Salonika; Serbia invaded **OCT**

Sebia collapses; British held in Mesopotamia at Ctesiphon **NOV**

Siege of Kut; Haig becomes BEF commander **DEC**

Top: German High Command—from left to right: Hindenburg, the Kaiser, Ludendorff.

Bottom: From left to right: French Minister of Munitions, Albert Thomas; Sir Douglas Haig; General Joffre; Lloyd George who was British Minister of Munitions and then Secretary for War.

26

General: Great fire in Constantinople.

Italian Front: In the Adriatic Italian troops capture Pelagosa Island.

War at sea: In the Adriatic French ships destroy an Austrian submarine supply station in Lagosta.

27

Eastern Front: Warsaw under direct attack on three sides.

Western Front: Soissons and Reims bombarded by German artillery.

The frontier between Italy and Austria. Many battles took place along the Isonzo river.

29

War at sea: In the Dardanelles the French submarine Mariotte is lost.

30

Eastern Front: Russians fall back all along the Eastern Front: only resisting north of Grusbieszow on the slopes of the Lower Bug.

Far East: Japanese cabinet resigns because of the political crisis.

Middle East: Cholera epidemic among Turkish troops in Constantinople.

Western Front: Germans use flame-throwers and break the British line at Hooge. Freiburg, Pzalzburg, and Pechelbronn bombed by 45 French planes.

73

1915

First use of gas
(on Eastern Front
in Poland)
JAN

Palestine
and Gallipoli
Fronts open
FEB

Russian offensive in
east; BEF attacks at
Neuve Chappelle
in west
MAR

Gallipoli landings;
Germans use gas
at Ypres
APR

Sinking of Lusitania;
first zeppelin raid
on London
MAY

Italian Front
opens
J

French scout in a shattered wood near Verdun.

31
Western Front: End of 10-day movement of German troops from the Eastern Front to the Western Front.

Politics: Bulgaria announces that it will neither join the Central Powers nor attack Serbia.

August 1915
After incurring world revulsion and in particular American anger German high command announces that they are restricting submarine attacks against non-military shipping. The Allies continue their disastrous Gallipoli campaign. In August alone the Allies lost 40,000 soldiers – mostly from Australia and New Zealand – either killed in action or to dysentry and disease.

2
Eastern Front: Germans claim to have captured 9,000 Russians during their latest retreat.

War at sea: In the Baltic a British submarine sinks a German transport ship carrying troops for von Below's army.

Western Front: Fighting around the Argonne and Verdun regions.

4
Eastern Front: The Russians evacuate Ivangorod while the Germans threaten Warsaw.

5
Caucasus: The Russians capture Turkish positions near Sarikamish and Olti.

Russia retreats from Poland; Germany surrenders in SW Africa **JUL**

Germans occupy Warsaw **AUG**

Champagne and Artois-Loos offensives in west **SEP**

Allies land in Salonika; Serbia invaded **OCT**

Sebia collapses; British held in Mesopotamia at Ctesiphon **NOV**

Siege of Kut; Haig becomes BEF commander **DEC**

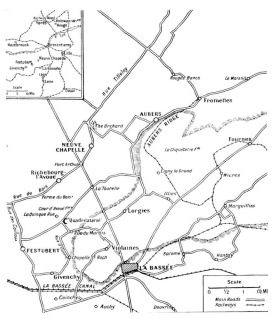

The military cemetery near the entrance to Fort St Michel, near Verdun.

Bottom: HMS Queen Elizabeth leads Colossus, St Vincent and Bellerophon.

Eastern Front: Germans enter Warsaw and cpature Ivangorod.

Western Front: Heavy fighting in the Vosges.

6

Gallipoli: Battle of Sari Bair begins. A diversionary attack is made while two Allied reinforcement divisions make a surprise landing at Suvla Bay and attack Achi Baba on the west of the peninsula.

7

Eastern Front: Fierce fighting all over the Eastern Front. Russians retreat behind the Jara and hold off the Germans in the Riga region.

Gallipoli: Relentless fighting in blisteringly hot weather totals up heavy losses.

District north of La Bassée showing Aubers Ridge and Festubert where the British attacked German positions in May 1915. Inset, the larger area showing Ypres to Lens.

Western Front: Allies repulse German attacks in the Vosges and Argonne. The latter taking heavy losses.

8

Eastern Front: German troops under Mackensen force the Russians back over the Veprj.

Italian Front: In the north Adriatic Monfalcone dockyard is bombed.

War at sea: The German High Seas Fleet attack in the Gulf of Riga.
HMS Ramsay is sunk by the German steamer Meteor.
AMC India of the Northern Patrol is mined off Bodo, Norway.

First use of gas (on Eastern Front in Poland) **JAN**

Palestine and Gallipoli Fronts open **FEB**

Russian offensive in east; BEF attacks at Neuve Chappelle in west **MAR**

Gallipoli landings; Germans use gas at Ypres **APR**

Sinking of Lusitania; first zeppelin raid on London **MAY**

Italian Front opens J

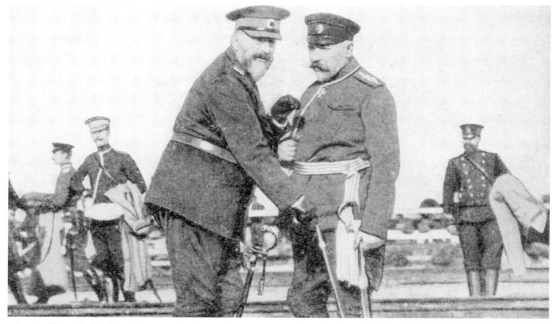

King Ferdinand of Bulgaria in consultation with General Ivanoff.

9

Caucasus: 255,000 Armenians arrive from Van.

Eastern Front: Osovyets is evacuated and then destroyed by the Russians.

Gallipoli: In the Dardanelles Anzac troops are taking heavy losses.

War at sea: German auxiliary minelayer Meteor scuttled to avoid capture by Harwich Force cruisers 50 miles northwest of Horns Reef.
Turkish battleship Kheir-ed-Din Barbarossa is torpedoed by a British submarine.
HMS Lynx hits a mine and sinks.

Western Front: A German Zeppelin raids the east coast of England: another is destroyed at Dunkirk.

12

Balkans: Serbians bomb Semlin and Panchevo in retaliation for Austrian bombing of Belgrade.

Great Britain: A Zeppelin raid on the east coast of England leaves 29 victims.

Middle East: German munition factory at Jaffa is shelled and destroyed by a French cruiser.

War at sea: German and Russian fleets engage near Riga.

14

War at sea: In the Aegean the transport ship Royal Edward is sunk: 800 drown and 600 are saved.

Russia retreats from Poland; Germany surrenders in SW Africa **JUL**

Germans occupy Warsaw **AUG**

Champagne and Artois-Loos offensives in west **SEP**

Allies land in Salonika; Serbia invaded **OCT**

Sebia collapses; British held in Mesopotamia at Ctesiphon **NOV**

Siege of Kut; Haig becomes BEF commander **DEC**

Italian machine-gun post watches the skies.
Bottom: Gas masks on Germans captured during a gas attack.

Western Front: Valley of Spada (on the Meuse) bombarded by 19 French planes.

15

Italian Front: Venice bombed by enemy seaplane.

Western Front: Violent bombardments along Yser front.

16

Western Front: Towns along the coast of England in Cumberland are shelled by German submarine.

17

Eastern Front: Fall of Kovna as Russians lose heavily despite fierce fighting on the Eastern Front.
Germany claims to have taken two million

Italian 280mm gun.

prisoners, over three quarters of them Russians.

18

War at sea: German fleet withdraws from Gulf of Riga having lost two cruisers and eight torpedo boats: Russians lost the gunboat Sivuch.

19

Eastern Front: Fall of Novo Gregievsk. Russians losing ground all over Eastern Front. Russians destroy a German landing force at Pernau, Riga.

War at sea: White Star liner Arabic torpedoed and sunk by submarine off Fastnet, Ireland: 44 lives lost including two Americans. In neutral Danish waters British submarine E13 shelled when grounded.

1915

JAN — First use of gas (on Eastern Front in Poland)

FEB — Palestine and Gallipoli Fronts open

MAR — Russian offensive in east; BEF attacks at Neuve Chappelle in west

APR — Gallipoli landings; Germans use gas at Ypres

MAY — Sinking of Lusitania; first zeppelin raid on London

J — Italian Front opens

Below: German storm troopers on the Eastern Front holding a shallow line of pits before advancing.

20

Middle East: In Constantinople Russian planes bomb Topkhaneh arsenal.

Politics: Italy declares war on Turkey.

21

Gallipoli: Second Anzac attack in Suvla Bay on Anafarta is repulsed.
Start of the Battle of Scimitar Hill. The last major Allied offensive on the Gallipoli Front. Allies make no gains but lose 5,000 casualties.

United States: U.S. newspaper report in the Washington Post says that contingency plans are being drawn up to send a million soldiers to the war in Europe.

War at sea: The German fleet gives up its attempt to take Riga and withdraws.

22

Eastern Front: The city of Osovyets falls to the Germans.

War at sea: Near Ostend a German destroyer is sunk by two French torpedo boats.

23

War at sea: Turkish supply ship Isfahan torpedoed by British submarine near Constantinople.

24

United States: The U.S. War College Division denies Washington Post and Baltimore Sun allegations of plans to send American soldiers to join the war.

Western Front: Start of 13-day continuous artillery duel on the Western Front.

ssia retreats from Poland; Germany surrenders in SW Africa **JUL**

Germans occupy Warsaw **AUG**

Champagne and Artois-Loos offensives in west **SEP**

Allies land in Salonika; Serbia invaded **OCT**

Sebia collapses; British held in Mesopotamia at Ctesiphon **NOV**

Siege of Kut; Haig becomes BEF commander **DEC**

Top: Zeppelin towed into Ostend harbour after being hit by British AA fire.

.Bottom: Gas attack warning

.Preparing wire for transport to the front

25

Caucasus: Reports reach the outside world of horrorfying massacres in Armenia.

Eastern Front: The Russian fortress of Brest-Litovsk is stormed and taken by Austro-German forces.

26

Western Front: French planes bomb the poison gas factory at Dornach.

27

Balkans: German troops start to gather near the Romanian northwest frontier.

War at sea: Handelskrieg – 'trade warfare' – is given up. German submarines are forbidden to attack passenger ships without

warning and to give the crew time to abandon ship: for fear of antagonizing the Americans further.

Western Front: Allies take German trenches at Landersbach and Sondernach in Alsace.

28

Italian Front: Italians reach and take Monte Cista in Trentino.

30

Eastern Front: Russian victory at Strypa in southern Galicia: capture 4,000 prisoners.

Great Britain: British deaths from Zeppelin raids over England are given as 89 civilians.

Middle East: British submarine attacks Constantinople and in the process damages the Galata Bridge.

First use of gas
(on Eastern Front
in Poland)
JAN

Palestine
and Gallipoli
Fronts open
FEB

Russian offensive in
east; BEF attacks at
Neuve Chappelle
in west
MAR

Gallipoli landings;
Germans use gas
at Ypres
APR

Sinking of Lusitania;
first zeppelin raid
on London
MAY

Italian Front
opens
J

Airmen were renowned for their courage: in the centre is Canadian Lt-Col Avery Bishop who took part in 170 air battles during which he shot down 72 German planes. He was awarded the VC, DSO and bar, MC and DFC.

31

Western Front: Germany claims victory in the Vosges.

September 1915

Stalemate on the Western Front despite fierce fighting. With Russia largely withdrawn from the Eastern Front in Poland the Central Powers turn their might to attacking Serbia.

1

Eastern Front: Germans attack Grodno. Austrians enter Brody.

War at sea: Official German start date of cessation of sinking passenger ships without warning.

2

Eastern Front: After fierce fighting Grodno falls to Austro-German troops. Fierce fighting around Vilna.

Politics: General Polivanov becomes Prime Minister of Russia.

War at sea: In Gallipoli British submarines sink four Turkish transports off Akbachi Sliman and Nagara.
In the Aegean the British transport Southland is torpedoed.

3

Eastern Front: General von Beseler appointed Governor General of Russian Poland.
Russian forces retake Grodno and hold the line between the Dniester and the Pripet Marshes.

Russia retreats from Poland; Germany surrenders in SW Africa
JUL

Germans occupy Warsaw
AUG

Champagne and Artois-Loos offensives in west
SEP

Allies land in Salonika; Serbia invaded
OCT

Sebia collapses; British held in Mesopotamia at Ctesiphon
NOV

Siege of Kut; Haig becomes BEF commander
DEC

The merchant ship has been holed by a torpedo in the bows from the German submarine on the left. The crew have been evacuated and the U-boat is about to sink the ship.

Bottom: German U-boat firing across the bows of a merchant vessel warning her to surrender before being sunk.

4

War at sea: Off the Irish coast the liner Hesperian is torpedoed: she later sinks with the loss of 32 lives.

5

Eastern Front: Czar Nicholas II of Russia becomes Commander-in-Chief of the Russian armies replacing Grand Duke Nicholas whose command is transferred to the Caucasus. General Alexeiev becomes Commander in the South and General Russki takes over the Northern Army.

Western Front: Continuous heavy artillery action along the Western Front, especially in the Arras region.

Two battleships of the Grand Fleet in the North Sea — the guns belong to Queen Elizabeth and following her is the Orion.

6

Africa: In German East Africa fighting betweenGermans and Belgians near Saisa on the Rhodesian frontier.

Italian Front: Fighting between Austrians and Italians.

War at sea: In the Sea of Marmora Turkish destroyer Yar Hissar sunk by submarine.

Western Front: Saarbrücken is bombed by 40 French planes.
The British assess a prototype tank for suitability for use on the Western Front.

7

Eastern Front: Austrian troops take Dubno and control the railroad from Riga to Lemberg (Lvov).

81

First use of gas (on Eastern Front in Poland)
JAN

Palestine and Gallipoli Fronts open
FEB

Russian offensive in east; BEF attacks at Neuve Chappelle in west
MAR

Gallipoli landings; Germans use gas at Ypres
APR

Sinking of Lusitania; first zeppelin raid on London
MAY

Italian Front opens

Supply column following up the German advance on the road to Brest-Litowsk in Poland.

Great Britain: Zeppelin raid on the east coast of England kills 7 and injures 50.

War at sea: British and French fleets bombard the Belgian coast at Ostend and Westeinde.

8

Eastern Front: Russian victory at Tarnopol and Trembovla: they take 8,000 prisoners.

War at sea: In the eastern Mediterranean off the island of Rhodes, the French auxiliary cruiser Indien torpedoed.

Great Britain: Zeppelins raid London and the east coast of England: 20 killed and 86 wounded.

Western Front: German offensive in the Argonne renewed.

9

Mesopotamia: In Shiraz, Persia, the British Vice-Consul is wounded and dies. German conspiracy is suspected.

Western Front: Heavy fighting continues in the Vosges.

12

Eastern Front: The Vilna-Dvinsk railroad is cut near Svyentsyani by Austro-German troops.

General: Following poor Austrian leadership Germany assumes ultimate control of Austro-Hungarian forces.

War at sea: The Belgian Relief Ship Pomona is sunk.

Russia retreats from Poland; Germany surrenders in SW Africa **JUL**

Germans occupy Warsaw **AUG**

Champagne and Artois-Loos offensives in west **SEP**

Allies land in Salonika; Serbia invaded **OCT**

Sebia collapses; British held in Mesopotamia at Ctesiphon **NOV**

Siege of Kut; Haig becomes BEF commander **DEC**

Struggle for the possession of Kut in September 1915. Bottom: German wiring party.

Romania, showing the opening stages of the campaigns. The country was threatened by Austrians to the north and west, and by Germans, Turks and Bulgars in the south-east.

Western Front: Heavy bombardments on the French front.

13

Politics: Bulgarian and Macedonian men are called up.

United States: Newspaper reports in the U.S. press talk of German sabotage in factories and political intrigue.

17

Eastern Front: Russians are beaten back and Russian army withdraws to positions between the rivers Vilna and Pripet.

18

Eastern Front: Vilna falls to the Germans and the Russians retreat towards Minsk.

War at sea: British fleet and French artillery bombard the Belgian coast.

19

War at sea: In the Aegean the British transport ship Ramazan sunk by submariine with the loss of 300 Indian troops.

21

Balkans: Anglo-French forces attack in Macedonia.
Bulgarian army ordered to mobilize for a situatiion of 'armed neutrality'.

Eastern Front: Fierce fighting around Dvinsk.

Politics: Dutch politicians reaffirm their neutrality.

Western Front: French successes in the Vosges at Hartmannsweilerkopf and along the Aisne-Marne canal.

First use of gas (on Eastern Front in Poland) **JAN**

Palestine and Gallipoli Fronts open **FEB**

Russian offensive in east; BEF attacks at Neuve Chappelle in west **MAR**

Gallipoli landings; Germans use gas at Ypres **APR**

Sinking of Lusitania; first zeppelin raid on London **MAY**

Italian Front opens

Tsar Nicholas and his cousin (right) the Grand Duke Nicholas.

22

Eastern Front: Russian forces successful everywhere on the Eastern Front except in the center.

Gallipoli: Anzac casualties in the Dardanelles listed as 4,604 dead and 19,183 injured.

War at sea: In the English Channel the Dutch liner Koningin Emma is mined. She is successfully towed up the Thames and 250 passengers saved.

Western Front: Second Battle of Champagne begins.

23

Eastern Front: In Minsk the Russians capture Vileika.
Russians take Lutsk and capture almost 12,000 prisoners.

Western Front: Entire front sees artillery activity.

25

Eastern Front: Germans take heavy losses attacking Dvinsk and withdraw.

War at sea: On Gulf of Riga Russian Fleet bombards German positions.

Western Front: Anglo-French offensive at Artois-Loos, begins the Battle of Loos. British deploy chlorine gas against the Germans but the wind changes and blows it over their own men.
Successful French attack in Champagne between Suippe and the Aisne.

26

Balkans: All Greeks are reported to have been expelled from Smyrna.

Russia retreats from Poland; Germany surrenders in SW Africa **JUL**

Germans occupy Warsaw **AUG**

Champagne and Artois-Loos offensives in west **SEP**

Allies land in Salonika; Serbia invaded **OCT**

Sebia collapses; British held in Mesopotamia at Ctesiphon **NOV**

Siege of Kut; Haig becomes BEF commander **DEC**

Top: German submarines U.35 and U.42 on the surface in the Mediterranean. The German authorities claimed that the former sank more tonnage of shipping than any other submarine.

Bottom: This British B.E. plane managed to get back behind Allied lines before attempting a forced landing. The pilot, observer and plane were all undamaged.

A British observer loading a machine-gun magazine onto his plane. His pilot controlled a fixed double gun that fired through the propeller.

War at sea: Italian battleship Benedetto Brin catches fire and explodes.

Western Front: French successes in Champagne capture 16,000 German prisoners.

Western Front: French victories in the Champagne region.

27
Western Front: British Guards regiment successful on Hill 70 at Loos.
German offensive in the Argonne is driven back.

29
Eastern Front: In Galicia fierce fighting on the Strypa River and southeast of Russian-held Dvinsk.

Western Front: Allied success as the French capture Vimy Ridge; as they advance through Champagne they take 23,000 prisoners.

28
Eastern Front: Battles in the Pripet Marshes: Germans sustain heavy losses.
Russian troops withdraw from Lutsk.

Middle East: Around the Tigris important British victory at Kut-el-Amara.

30
Eastern Front: On the Eastern Front the German advance grinds to a halt.

1915

First use of gas (on Eastern Front in Poland) **JAN**

Palestine and Gallipoli Fronts open **FEB**

Russian offensive in east; BEF attacks at Neuve Chappelle in west **MAR**

Gallipoli landings; Germans use gas at Ypres **APR**

Sinking of Lusitania; first zeppelin raid on London **MAY**

Italian Front opens **J**

German U-boat in mid-Atlantic takes on a torpedo and other supplies from its 'parent ship'.

Western Front: French continuing to be successful in Champagne region.

October 1915

The Balkan Front sees the main action of the month as Austrian and German troops invade Serbia.

1

Balkans: Austrian and German troops gather all along the border with Serbia.

Western Front: British monitors bombard Lombaertzyde and Middelkerke in Belgium.

3

Balkans: Bulgarian forces concentrate along their border.

Politics: Russia sends an ultimatum to Bulgaria to pull back from the Serbian border and stop cooperating with the Germans.

Western Front: French artillery bomb Metz.

5

Balkans: An Anglo-French force lands at Salonika in Greece to offer assistance to support Serbia. Within a couple of days they number 20,000. The Greek government resigns.
Bulgarian forces are being commanded by German officers.

6

Balkans: Triple Alliance – Germany, Bulgaria, Austria – troops attack Serbia from the north.

Politics: In Britain Parliament hears that an estimated 800,000 Armenians have been massacred with German assistance in the last six months.

Russia retreats from Poland; Germany surrenders in SW Africa **JUL**

Germans occupy Warsaw **AUG**

Champagne and Artois-Loos offensives in west **SEP**

Allies land in Salonika; Serbia invaded **OCT**

Serbia collapses; British held in Mesopotamia at Ctesiphon **NOV**

Siege of Kut; Haig becomes BEF commander **DEC**

Ten-days' leave tickets being waved in the air by happy troops at Poperinghe.

Bottom: General Luigi Cardona, commander-in-chief of Italian forces in 1915.

On the night of September 23, 1915, 12 zeppelins raided England. L33 was hit, crash-landed in Essex and was then destroyed by her crew.

7

Balkans: 400,000 Austro-German troops cross the rivers Danube, Drina, and Save.

Politics: New Greek administration announces its benevolent neutrality towards the Allies.

War at sea: Off the Anatolian coast two Russian destroyers sink 19 Turkish supply ships.

8

Balkans: Serbs evacuate Belgrade before Austro-German troops enter the city.

Western Front: Massive German losses as they attack in numbers at Loos.

9

Balkans: The Montenegrin frontier is attacked by Austrian troops.

Eastern Front: Russians are losing ground and taking heavy losses.

10

Balkans: In Belgrade many civilian inhabitants are killed by occupying troops.

War at sea: German metal steamer Lulea sunk by British submarine.

11

Balkans: Bulgarians attack Serbia from Byelogradchik; Belgrade is virtually destroyed.

Eastern Front: On the Strypa in Galicia 2,000 Austrians are captured by Ivanov's forces.

First use of gas (on Eastern Front in Poland) **JAN**

Palestine and Gallipoli Fronts open **FEB**

Russian offensive in east; BEF attacks at Neuve Chappelle in west **MAR**

Gallipoli landings; Germans use gas at Ypres **APR**

Sinking of Lusitania; first zeppelin raid on London **MAY**

Italian Front opens **JI**

The Salonika Front opened on October 5, 1915. The French and British fleet is seen here, with Greek soldiers in the foreground.

12

Balkans: Bulgaria declares war on Serbia.

Politics: Greece refuses to help Serbia despite their 1913 treaty. Says terms not triggered by current conflict.

Western Front: English nurse Edith Cavell shot by Germans for helping British prisoners to escape from Belgium to Holland. World opinion is outraged.

13

Great Britain: A Zeppelin raid on London kills 55 and injures a further 114.

14

United States: Congress agrees an increase in the size of the U.S. Army.

15

Balkans: Bulgarians occupy Vranya in Serbia.

Mesopotamia: In Persia Germans evacuate Kermanshah.

Politics: Great Britain declares war on Bulgaria.

16

Eastern Front: Heavy fighting in the Riga region.

Politics: France declares war on Bulgaria.

War at sea: In the Baltic a British submarine sinks five German transport ships.

18

Italian Front: Start of the Third Battle of the Isonzo.

JUL Russia retreats from Poland; Germany surrenders in SW Africa

AUG Germans occupy Warsaw

SEP Champagne and Artois-Loos offensives in west

OCT Allies land in Salonika; Serbia invaded

NOV Sebia collapses; British held in Mesopotamia at Ctesiphon

DEC Siege of Kut; Haig becomes BEF commander

British marines high above one of the Aegean Island strongholds

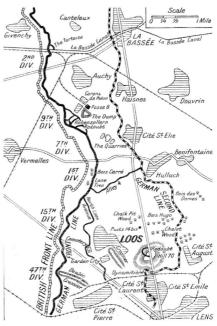

Area around Loos assaulted by the British towards the end of September, 1915. The map shows the German front and second lines of defence and the positions of the six British divisions involved in the main attack.

28

War at sea: Cruiser HMS Argyll grounded and lost off Dundee, Scotland.

29

Politics: The French Prime Minister M. Vivani is succeeded by M. Briand.

November 1915

As the cold weather sets in the Western Front becomes largely static and remains so for the winter. The British advance in Mesopotamia is halted. The Serbian Army is forced to retreat as the more powerful central Powers armies push into Serbia.

5

Balkans: The Serbian capital of Nish is captured by Bulgarian troops after three days of fighting.

9

War at sea: In the Mediterranean the Italian liner Ancona is shelled and sunk by German submarine, killing 272, some of them American.

10

Italian Front: Start of the Fourth Battle of the Isonzo.

21

Balkans: Fall of Novi-Bazar in Serbia to Austro-German troops.

22

Mesopotamia: In Persia, Allies beat the Turks at the Battle of Ctesiphon, about 25 miles south of Bagdad.

1915

JAN — First use of gas (on Eastern Front in Poland)

FEB — Palestine and Gallipoli Fronts open

MAR — Russian offensive in east; BEF attacks at Neuve Chappelle in west

APR — Gallipoli landings; Germans use gas at Ypres

MAY — Sinking of Lusitania; first zeppelin raid on London

J — Italian Front opens

Bulgarians advance into Serbia.

23

Balkans: German, Austro-Hungarian and Bulgarian forces push the Serbian army into exile; Serbia falls.
Fall of Mitrovitsa, the temporary capital of Serbia, taking 17,000 prisoners.

24

Balkans: Serbian government transferred to Scutari, Albania. The Serbian people and their army attempt to evacuate the country by fleeing west across the mountains towards Albania. Many Serb soldiers and civilians die on this arduous journey.

25

Balkans: The Allies make Salonika the base of their Southern Front operations – with Greek government approval.

29

War at sea: In the Black Sea German submarine UC13 driven aground during a storm and stranded.

December 1915

The Gallipoli Campaign is an acknowledged disaster and the Allied withdrawal starts. The Allies agree regularly to consult on strategy.

4

Politics: Henry Ford, with large party of peace advocates, sets sail for Europe on steamer Oscar II, with the intention of ending the war.

5

Balkans: General Vassich orders the evacuation of Monastir.

Mesopotamia: Start of the Siege of Kut when four Turkish divisions surround the town.

Russia retreats from Poland; Germany surrenders in SW Africa **JUL**

Germans occupy Warsaw **AUG**

Champagne and Artois-Loos offensives in west **SEP**

Allies land in Salonika; Serbia invaded **OCT**

Serbia collapses; British held in Mesopotamia at Ctesiphon **NOV**

Siege of Kut; Haig becomes BEF commander **DEC**

Salonika area showing the line from the river Struma to Albania held by the British, French, Italian, Russian and Serbian troops.

Bottom: Djemal Pasha, leader of Turkish forces in Palestine and Sinai, points out locations on a map.

Contingent of Russian troops resting by the roadside while on their way to the front in Salonika in 1915.

6
Western Front: In Paris the first meeting of the Allied War council is held.

8
Gallipoli: Start of the evacuation of the Allies from Gallipoli towards the Greek frontier.

9
Balkans: On the Southern Front the Allies start to retreat from Vardar.

10
Gallipoli: The Allies begin slowly withdrawing from Gallipoli; they complete by January 9 1916.

13
Balkans: Serbia in hands of enemy, Allied forces abandoning last positions and retiring across Greek frontier.

15
Western Front: General Sir Douglas Haig succeeds Field Marshal Sir John French as Commander-in-Chief of British forces in France.

18
Western Front: Battle of Verdun ends with 550,000 French and 450,000 German casualties.

20
Gallipoli: Anzac troops start to secretly withdraw from positions on Suvla Bay and on the Gallipoli Peninsula.

1916

Retreat from
Gallipoli
JAN

German Verdun
offensive starts
FEB

Unrestricted U-boat
warfare begins again;
Sussex torpedoed
MAR

Easter Rising
in Ireland
APR

Crucial sea Battle of
Jutland; German fleet
returns to harbour
for rest of war
MAY

Arab Revolt takes
Mecca; US/Mex
clash at Carr
J

King Peter of Serbia retreats into Greece.

Politics: Central Powers issue the Falkenhayn Memorandum which announces their intention to 'bleed the French white' through a war of attrition.

22
War at sea: Japanese liner Yasaka Maru lost.

31
War at sea: Cruiser Natal blows up in Cromarty Firth.

1916

January 1916

The Allied withdrawal from the Dardanelles is completed and the Gallipoli Front closes. In the USA popular fears about German sabotage get stronger especially when the suspicions are confirmed about Germany's attempts to keep the American public anti-war.

1
Africa: In the Cameroons the Allies take Yaounda.

Eastern Front: Major Russian offensive on the rivers Strypa and Styr.

4
Mesopotamia: The Battle of Sheikh Sa'ad is the first Anglo-Indian attempt to relieve the siege of Kut.

5
Balkans: Austria goes on the offensive in Montenegro and invades the country.

8
Gallipoli: Evacuation of Helles. Completed the following day.

Somme offensive in west: 60,000 British casualties on first day **JUL**

Romania joins war on Allied side **AUG**

First use of tanks at Flers-Courcelette **SEP**

French counteroffensive at Verdun **OCT**

Lawrence of Arabia joins Arab army; end of Somme offensive **NOV**

Romania beaten; President Wilson's peace note published **DEC**

Painting showing the sinking of the hospital ship Anglia, November 18, 1915, after it struck a mine in the English Channel.

10

Caucasus: Russia starts the Erzurum Offensive in the Armenian Caucasus.

11

Balkans: The Greek island of Corfu is occupied by the French.

13

Balkans: Cettinje, the capital of Montenegro, is occupied by Austrians.

Mesopotamia: Battle of Hanna – the second Anglo-Indian attempt to raise the siege of Kut – fails.

15

United States: U.S. German naval attache Von Papen's papers are published – his check counter-foils show his payments to German agents operating in the U.S.

War at sea: Admiral Reinhardt Scheer is given command of the German High Seas Fleet.

16

Balkans: In Salonika General Sarrail takes command.

Caucasus: The Russians launch a major offensive.

24

General: Conscription is introduced in Britain with the passing of the Military Service Act in Parliament, it becomes law in February.

25

Balkans: Montenegro accepts Austrian surrender terms.

1916

JAN — Retreat from Gallipoli

FEB — German Verdun offensive starts

MAR — Unrestricted U-boat warfare begins again; Sussex torpedoed

APR — Easter Rising in Ireland

MAY — Crucial sea Battle of Jutland; German fleet returns to harbour for rest of war

J... — Arab Revolt takes Mecca; US/Me... clash at Car...

Serbian artillery tries to cover the retreat of the Serbian Army in the face of the Austrians.

27
United States: President Wilson makes three speeches in New York and starts a nationwide whistle-stop campaign to generate support for joining the European war.

29
Western Front: Campaign to bomb Paris and towns in England by Zeppelins begins.

31
United States: The U.S. War College Division warns its employees 'to engage in no discussion whatever concerning the progress of the European War.'

February 1916
With spring on the way Germany launches huge offensives on the Western Front. British munitions minister, David Lloyd George, approves full production of the first tank.

3
United States: U.S. President Wilson delivers final speech of his Preparedness Campaign in Saint Louis.

7
Western Front: The RFC forms its first single-seat fighter squadron — No. 24 — flying Airco DH2s.

8
War at sea: French cruiser Admiral Charner is torpedoed off the Syrian coast by U-21: 374 lives lost.

9
Politics: Military Service Act becomes law in Britain allowing conscription.

10
War at sea: Minesweeping sloop Arabis is

JUL — Somme offensive in west. 60,000 British casualties on first day

AUG — Romania joins war on Allied side

SEP — First use of tanks at Flers-Courcelette

OCT — French counteroffensive at Verdun

NOV — Lawrence of Arabia joins Arab army; end of Somme offensive

DEC — Romania beaten; President Wilson's peace note published

Top: Retreat from Suvla Bay.

Commander-in-chief of the British armies in France, Sir Douglas Haig, seen in the special train placed at his disposal in France.

Armenia, most of Mesopotamia and the north of Persia — the areas fought over by the Russians and Turks in the winter of 1915-16.

sunk by German destroyers east of the Dogger Bank. Grand Fleet and Harwich Force are ordered out of port to search for the enemy.

11

War at sea: Returning Harwich Force flagship Arethusa mined off Harwich.

16

Caucasus: In Armenia the Russians capture Erzerum, taking 13,000 prisoners. Large numbers of Arabs desert from the Turkish Army.

18

Africa: German troops in Cameroon surrender at Mora to British, French, and Belgian troops attacking from neighboring colonies.

21

Western Front: The Battle of Verdun starts with a German attack on Mort-Homme ridge, west of Verdun. The fighting lasts for ten months until 6 December and claims over a million casualties.

23

Western Front: French artillery kills the entire French 72nd division at Samogneux, Verdun.

24

United States: U.S. Acting Secretary of War, Hugh L. Scott asks the United States War College Division what plans have been made in the event of a 'complete rupture' with Germany.

Western Front: Marshal Pétain is given command of the defense of Verdun.

1916

Retreat from
Gallipoli
JAN

German Verdun
offensive starts
FEB

Unrestricted U-boat
warfare begins again;
Sussex torpedoed
MAR

Easter Rising
in Ireland
APR

Crucial sea Battle of
Jutland; German fleet
returns to harbour
for rest of war
MAY

Arab Revolt takes
Mecca; US/Me**
clash at Car*

Marseilles—Scots troops en route from India to the Western Front, 1916.

25
Western Front: Fort Douaumont falls to Germans and the French are driven out during the battle of Verdun. 500 soldiers are either killed or injured.

26
War at sea: German commerce raider Wolf runs aground in the Elbe Estuary and heavily damaged, decommissioned as a raider. German submarine sinks the French transport ship Provence II, killing 930.

27
War at sea: In the Straits of Dover P&O liner Maloja is blown up by a mine: 155 lost.

29
War at sea: British auxilary ship Alcantara sunk in action with German raider Greif 70 miles northeast of the Shetlands. The badly damaged Grief finished off by other Royal Navy forces.

March 1916
The German attack on Verdun eventually falters and fails to make a breakthrough. The German unrestricted campaign against shipping is resumed, even at the risk of alienating American opinion.

1
War at sea: Germany starts an 'unlimited' submarine campaign to break Britain by starving her of food and supplies and by destroying British shipping.
In the Mediterranean HMS Primula is torpedoed.

6
United States: Pacifist Democratic lawyer Newton Baker is made U.S. secretary for war.

Somme offensive in west: 60,000 British casualties on first day **JUL**

Romania joins war on Allied side **AUG**

First use of tanks at Flers-Courcelette **SEP**

French counteroffensive at Verdun **OCT**

Lawrence of Arabia joins Arab army; end of Somme offensive **NOV**

Romania beaten; President Wilson's peace note published **DEC**

Russian troops freshly arrived from Siberia being reviewed by their commander-in-chief, General Sarrail, in Salonika.

Bottom: French grenadiers.

Women took on many jobs after conscription was introduced in 1916.

9

Italian Front: Fifth Battle of the Isonzo starts.

Politics: Germany declares war on Portugal on the latter's refusal to give up seized ships.

United States: Pancho Villa's raid on Columbus, New Mexico. Pancho Villa leads 1,500 Mexican raiders in an attack against Columbus, New Mexico, killing 17.

11

Italian Front: 5th, 6th, 7th, 8th and 9th Battles of Isonzo between Italy and Austria-Hungary are rugularly launched until 14 November.

12

Italian Front: The Fifth Italian Isonzo Offensive, lasts until the 29th.

13

Africa: In German East Africa the British led by General Smuts start the major Morogoro Offensive.

15

Politics: Austria-Hungary declares war on Portugal.

United States: President Woodrow Wilson sends 12,000 U.S. troops led by General Pershing over the Mexican border to pursue Pancho Villa into Mexico.

16

War at sea: Off Harwich the Dutch liner Tubantia is torpedoed without warning. Admiral Alfred von Tirpitz resigns as Prussian navy minister in protest at restrictions on U-boat activity. Replaced by Admiral Eduard von Capelle.

Retreat from Gallipoli **JAN**

German Verdun offensive starts **FEB**

Unrestricted U-boat warfare begins again; Sussex torpedoed **MAR**

Easter Rising in Ireland **APR**

Crucial sea Battle of Jutland, German fleet returns to harbour for rest of war **MAY**

Arab Revolt takes Mecca, US/Me clash at Ca

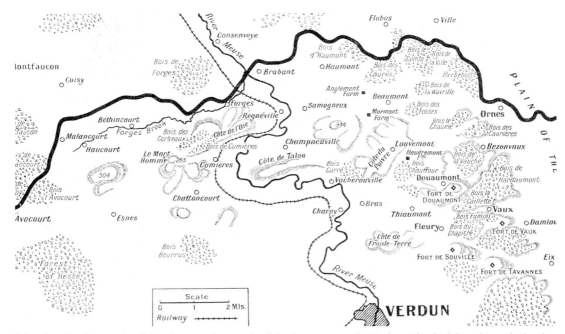

Map showing the terrain of the nine-month struggle of the Germans to take Verdun. The thick line shows the battle front as of 21 February 1916.

18

Eastern Front: Start of the first Battle of Lake Naroch.

19

United States: First U.S. air combat mission as eight American planes take off in pursuit of Pancho Villa.

24

War at sea: French cross-channel steamer Sussex is sunk by a torpedo from a German submarine off Dieppe with many Americans aboard. 50 lives are lost but no Americans die.

25

War at sea: HMS Cleopatria sinks a German destroyer.
Following a collision in the North Sea the destroyer HMS Medusa sinks.

31

Western Front: Melancourt taken by Germans in the Battle of Verdun.

April 1916

British forces in Mesopotamia begin to advance on Baghdad but fail to relieve Kut-el-Amara. The United States compels Germany to stop unrestricted submarine warfare.

4

Eastern Front: Alexi Brusilov is given command of Russia's Southern Front.

United States: American naval and military attaches in Paris and London draft plan for mobilizing US shipping to carry an American army to Europe, but their plan is ignored (this plan did not survive, but is referred to in a memorandum of 14 November 1916, Record of the Joint Army and Navy Board).

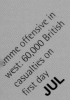
Somme offensive in west: 60,000 British casualties on first day **JUL**

Romania joins war on Allied side **AUG**

First use of tanks at Flers-Courcelette **SEP**

French counteroffensive at Verdun **OCT**

Lawrence of Arabia joins Arab army; end of Somme offensive **NOV**

Romania beaten; President Wilson's peace note published **DEC**

Former luxury liner Braemar Castle in hospital ship livery at quayside in Salonika as she embarks wounded soldiers to take back to Britain.

Bottom: The Grand Fleet at Scapa Flow. In the foreground HMS Royal Oak.

Marshal Pétain, one of the great French commanders of the First World War, seen before he was promoted to chief of staff in 1917

5

Mesopotamia: First Battle of Kut — third and final attempt by the British to raise the siege of Kut and rescue the British garrison.

7

Caucasus: Supported and covered by the Black Sea Fleet 16,000 Russian troops land on the Turkish coast at Rize to support Allied operations in the area.

9

Mesopotamia: A British attack on Turkish positions at Sanna-I-Yat fails.

Western Front: New German offensive at Verdun.

12

United States: A plot is discovered in the U.S. to blow up munitions ships.

15

Mesopotamia: First use of aircraft for delivering food and supplies when RFC and RNAS aircraft carry 13 tons of stores to Allied 9,000 men holding beseiged Kut-el-Amara from the Turks.

18

Caucasus: Russian troops take Trebizond.

19

War at sea: U.S. President Wilson calls for Germany to stop their submarine policy of sinking all ships in enemy waters without warning. This follows the sinking of the Sussex on 24 March.

1916

Retreat from Gallipoli
JAN

German Verdun offensive starts
FEB

Unrestricted U-boat warfare begins again; Sussex torpedoed
MAR

Easter Rising in Ireland
APR

Crucial sea Battle of Jutland; German fleet returns to harbour for rest of war
MAY

Arab Revolt takes Mecca; US/Me— clash at Car
J

British artillerymen forced to pull their own due to the lack of transport animals and the impassability of the ground for vehicles.

20
War at sea: Germany stops unrestricted U-boat attacks against shipping.

Western Front: Russian troops land at Marseilles in southern France for service on the French Front.

24
Politics: The Easter Rising — Irish rebellion against British rule in Ireland — begins in Dublin. The Irish Republic declared and Patrick Pearse appointed first President.

25
War at sea: German battlecruisers bombard Yarmouth and Lowestoft.

27
United States: Marshal Lord Kitchener, the British Secretary of State for War, asks America to send troops and participate in the war in Europe.

29
Mesopotamia: In Kut-el-Amara British forces under General Townshend surrender to the Turks after 146 days of siege. 3,000 British and 6,000 Indian soldiers are taken prisoner.

30
Politics: The Irish rebellion ends with the unconditional surrender of Pearse and other leaders, who are tried by court-martial.

May 1916
The Italian mainland is invaded by the Austrian army. On the Western Front the fighting at Verdun intensifies. Russia wins victories in the Caucasus. At sea, the most significant battle of the war takes place in the North Sea. At Jutland, 274 ships and over

JUL Somme offensive in west: 60,000 British casualties on first day

AUG Romania joins war on Allied side

SEP First use of tanks at Flers-Courcelette

OCT French counteroffensive at Verdun

NOV Lawrence of Arabia joins Arab army; end of Somme offensive

DEC Romania beaten; President Wilson's peace note published

The Sussex was struck by a torpedo in the bows. Here she is in Boulogne harbour.

Bivouac of French colonial troops from Cochin, China who were fighting with the Allies based in Salonika and commanded by General Sarrail.

70,000 men of the German High Seas Fleet and the British Grand Fleet fight for control of the North Sea. While the Germans sink more ships, the British win the strategic battle and the German fleet returns to harbour: it does not come out to fight the British again.

3

Politics: Britain executes 15 leaders of the Easter Rising between 3rd and 12th, turning the men into Republican heroes and martyrs.

4

War at sea: Germany renounces submarine policy. Germany makes the 'Sussex Pledge' to the U.S. promising to stop sinking merchant ships without warning; however, they add that this promise isn't permanent.

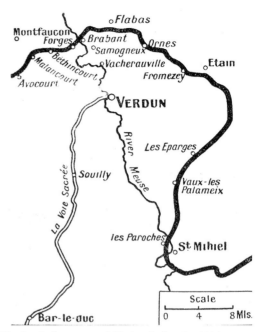

The battle front around Verdun before the 1916 German offensive.

8

War at sea: The White Star liner Cymrio torpedoed off the Irish coast.

14

Italian Front: Start of the Battle of the Trentino: Austrian troops mount an offensive against Italy on the Trentino Front.

15

Italian Front: Start of the Battle of Asiago. Start of the Trentino Offensive.

Western Front: Severe fighting on Vimy Ridge.

19

Politics: Britain and France conclude Sykes-Picot agreement.

101

1916

Retreat from
Gallipoli
JAN

German Verdun
offensive starts
FEB

Unrestricted U-boat
warfare begins again;
Sussex torpedoed
MAR

Easter Rising
in Ireland
APR

Crucial sea Battle of
Jutland; German fleet
returns to harbour
for rest of war
MAY

Arab Revolt takes
Mecca; US/Mex
clash at Carr
J

Australian troops wave to the camera as they march up to the front line.

25
General: In Britain the Military Service Act comes into effect.

26
Balkans: Bulgarians invade Greece and occupy forts on the Struma.

31
War at sea: Battle of Jutland — the only major naval battle of the war — begins. The British lost three battlecruisers — the Invincible, the Queen Mary, and the Indefatigable — plus three cruisers, eight destroyers, and 6,100 men. The Germans lost one battleship, one battlecruiser, four cruisers, and five destroyers, with 2,550 casualties. Following sinking of French steamer Sussex, Germany again agrees to 'visit and search' rules, insists that Great Britain should obey international laws on freedom of the seas.

June 1916
The Austro-Hungarian Army is destroyed on the Southern Front by Russian activity and Turkish forces, led by Enver Pasha, are defeated by the Russians in the Caucasus. Germany's Verdun offensive grinds to a halt following General Brusilov's highly successful Galician offensive which started on 4 June, forcing Germany to respond by diverting troops to the Eastern Front. The last Germany offensive in the battle for Verdun was launched at the end of June.

1
War at sea: End of the Battle of Jutland. Ultimately the British lost more ships and men but the German fleet turned back and remained in port for the rest of the war. The Allies' blockade continues. Both sides considered they had won a victory.

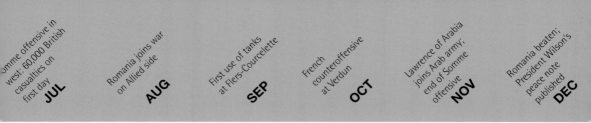

Somme offensive in west: 60,000 British casualties on first day **JUL**

Romania joins war on Allied side **AUG**

First use of tanks at Flers-Courcelette **SEP**

French counteroffensive at Verdun **OCT**

Lawrence of Arabia joins Arab army; end of Somme offensive **NOV**

Romania beaten; President Wilson's peace note published **DEC**

Torpedoed by a German submarine this merchant ship quickly sank.

Bottom: German soldier searching for British wounded among men and horses wiped out by a shell attack.

Behind German lines a British pilot and his plane have come to grief.

Russians take 13,000 prisoners on the first day and 12,000 the following.
Start of the Battle of Lutsk.

2

Western Front: Third Battle of Ypres starts with two German attacks on British trenches.

3

United States: National Defense Act authorizes the five-year expansion of U.S. Army, but at the same time drastically limits the size and authority of the U.S. War Department General Staff.

4

Eastern Front: Brusilov Offensive in Galicia and southern Russia (Carpathia). Massive Russian offensive launched front stretches from Pripet in Poland to the Romanian frontier. The assault is initially successful and the Austrian army takes heavy losses.

5

General: Lord Kitchener, British Secretary of War, dies when the cruiser HMS Hampshire is mined and sunk in high seas northwest of the Orkney Islands, Scotland. Kitchener and staff were journeying to Russia for discussions on the progress of the war.

Middle East: With British support (led by T.E. Lawrence), Hussein, grand sherif of Mecca, leads an Arab revolt against the Turks in the Hejaz. They were made promises of post-war independence against Ottoman rule.

6

Western Front: Germans capture Fort Vaux an attack on Verdun.

1916

Retreat from Gallipoli — JAN

German Verdun offensive starts — FEB

Unrestricted U-boat warfare begins again; Sussex torpedoed — MAR

Easter Rising in Ireland — APR

Crucial sea Battle of Jutland; German fleet returns to harbour for rest of war — MAY

Arab Revolt takes Mecca; US/Mex clash at Carr

Irish Guardsmen undergoing gas mask drill behind the lines on the Amiens-Albert road. They are wearing PH helmets fitted with goggles — they were later issued with box respirators.

7

Middle East: The Sherif of Mecca and other tribes of western and central Arabia withdraw their allegiance to the Ottoman Turks.

9

Italian Front: Italian counter-offensive ends the Battle of Trentino and starts a new phase.

16

Italian Front: As the Austrians suffer reversals the Italians launch a counter-offensive on the Asiago plateau.

17

Balkans: King Constantine of Greece orders the demobilization of the Greek army.

24

Western Front: British Somme offensive, a week-long artillery bombardment.

25

Eastern Front: Russia began offensive in eastern Galicia.

July 1916

Germany is forced to return to the defensive on the Western Front as the Allies take the initative. On the Southern Front the Russian advance in Galicia grinds to a halt.

1

Western Front: Battle of the Somme starts with an Anglo-French attack on a 25-mile front north and south of the Somme. The offensive starts with almost 750,000 soldiers attacking out of the trenches. 58,000 British troops are casualties on the first day, one third of them killed — the heaviest loss suffered by the British army in a single day during any war. The RFC establishes air superiority over the Somme and for some 30 miles behind,

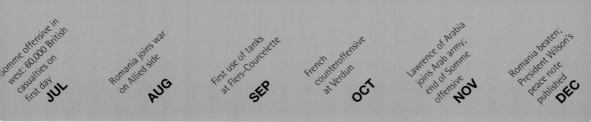

Somme offensive in west: 60,000 British casualties on first day **JUL**

Romania joins war on Allied side **AUG**

First use of tanks at Flers-Courcelette **SEP**

French counteroffensive at Verdun **OCT**

Lawrence of Arabia joins Arab army; end of Somme offensive **NOV**

Romania beaten; President Wilson's peace note published **DEC**

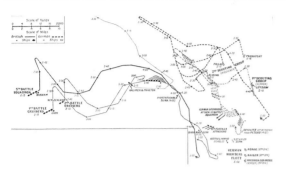

Diagram showing the courses of the British and German squadrons during the battle cruiser action before the main battle off Jutland.

Bottom: Marshal Fayolle, commander of the French 6th and 1st armies.

enemy lines. The offensive ended on 18 November with British army having taken its worst losses in history.

3

Western Front: The first RFC aircraft with a synchronized propeller/gun mechanism, the Sopwith 11/2 Strutter, becomes operational with 70 Squadron and takes part in the Battle of the Somme. The RFC has 27 squadrons with 421 aircraft and four kite balloon squadrons with 14 balloons assigned to support the British Army Corps.

4

Eastern Front: In the Ukraine the Russians under General Lesch launch the Second Great Russian Advance, driving the Austrians before them.

Commander-in-chief of the British Grand Fleet, Admiral Jellicoe.

War at sea: On the Black Sea Goeben and Breslau bombard Russian ports.

7

Africa: In German East Africa General Smuts occupies Tanga where the Usambara railroad terminates.

12

Eastern Front: On the Southern Front a furious Austrian attack on the Adige is driven back.

Western Front: The British gain Mametz Wood and also make progress through Trônes Wood.

14

Western Front: On the Somme, the British penetrate the German second line, using cavalry. Start of the Battle of Bazentin

Retreat from
Gallipoli
JAN

German Verdun
offensive starts
FEB

Unrestricted U-boat
warfare begins again;
Sussex torpedoed
MAR

Easter Rising
in Ireland
APR

Crucial sea Battle of
Jutland; German fleet
returns to harbour
for rest of war
MAY

Arab Revolt takes
Mecca; US/Mexico
clash at Carri
JU

Part of the German fleet en route to bombard Sunderland — however they met Beatty's battle cruiser squadron at Jutland instead.

Ridge. British capture Trônes Wood and take Longueval and Bazentin-le-Petit, so finishing the first phase of the Battle of the Somme.

15

Middle East: The Middle-East Brigade of the RFC is formed under the command of Brigadier General W G H Salmond, concentrating RFC units based in Macedonia, Mesopotamia, Palestine and East Africa under one command.

Western Front: British win the Battle of Delville Wood as they advance to penetrate Bois des Foureaux and the outskirts of Pozières.

19

Mesopotamia: Russian troops are driven back and defeated by the Turks.

22

United States: During a Preparedness Day parade in San Francisco, California, a bomb explodes on Market Street killing ten and injuring 40.

23

Western Front: Start of the Battle of Pozières Ridge.

25

Balkans: On the Salonika Front the reconstituted Serbian Army engages with the Bulgarians.

Caucasus: The Turks capture Erzingan in Armenia.

Western Front: Pozières occupied by British forces.

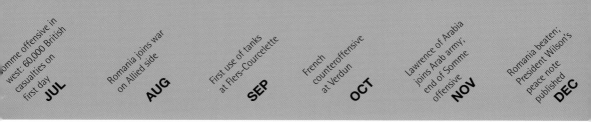

Somme offensive in west: 60,000 British casualties on first day **JUL**

Romania joins war on Allied side **AUG**

First use of tanks at Flers-Courcelette **SEP**

French counteroffensive at Verdun **OCT**

Lawrence of Arabia joins Arab army; end of Somme offensive **NOV**

Romania beaten; President Wilson's peace note published **DEC**

The German 25,000tons battlecruiser Seydlitz was badly damaged during the Battle of Jutland.

Bottom: The armour plating saved the Seydlitz from sinking at Jutland. She was later surrendered to the British and scuttled by her own crew at Scapa Flow in June 1919.

Admiral Sir David Beatty became commander-in-chief of the British Grand Fleet in November 1916.

27

Middle East: The Grand Sherif of Mecca captures Yanbo, the port of Medina.

28

Eastern Front: Sakharov enters Brody and takes 40,000 prisoners.

29

United States: U.S. Marines land in Haiti.

30

United States: Suspected German saboteurs blow up a munitions plant on Black Tom Island, in New York harbor. Tremors from the explosion are felt 90 miles away in Philadelphia.

August 1916

The fighting on the Somme although fierce did not see the front changing and the battle remained largely static with neither side making significant progress. Romania enters the war on the side of the Allies, but is quickly overrun by German forces. The fronts in Salonika and Palestine see activity again.

1

Italian Front: Fierce fighting on the Isonzo Front lasts for three days.

3

Middle East: Start of the Battle of Romani.

Western Front: French recapture Fleury.

107

1916

Retreat from Gallipoli
JAN

German Verdun offensive starts
FEB

Unrestricted U-boat warfare begins again; Sussex torpedoed
MAR

Easter Rising in Ireland
APR

Crucial sea Battle of Jutland; German fleet returns to harbour for rest of war
MAY

Arab Revolt takes Mecca; US/Mex clash at Carr
J

After a long day's march through summer heat, men of the Warwickshire Regiment collapse in near exhaustion before engaging in the battle of the Somme.

4
Africa: In East Africa the Belgians occupy Ujiji on Lake Tanganyika.

5
Middle East: In northern Sinai at Romani the British counter-attack and drive back the Turks, chasing them for 18 miles.

6
Italian Front: Start of the Battle of Gorizia as the Italians attack on the Isonzo starting the Sixth Battle of the Isonzo.

9
Italian Front: The Italians capture Gorizia and take 10,000 Austrain prisoners.

19
War at sea: Light cruisers HMSs Nottingham and Falmouth torpedoed and sunk.

20
Balkans: In Macedonia the Allies launch a general offensive.

24
Mesopotamia: Mush in Armenia is recaptured by the Russians.

26
Africa: In East Africa the British take and enter Morogoro.

27
Politics: Romania declares war on Austria-Hungary and the Central Powers and mobilizes her troops.

War at sea: Kaiser Wilhelm again restricts German submarine assaults to military shipping.

Somme offensive in west: 60,000 British casualties on first day **JUL**

Romania joins war on Allied side **AUG**

First use of tanks at Flers-Courcelette **SEP**

French counteroffensive at Verdun **OCT**

Lawrence of Arabia joins Arab army; end of Somme offensive **NOV**

Romania beaten; President Wilson's peace note published **DEC**

British soldiers preparing for the first bombardment which led to the battle of the Somme on 1 July 1916. The British batteries included 12- and 15in guns.

Bottom: Sir Henry Rawlinson, commander of the 4th army, conducted the opening offensive of the Somme in 1916.

28
Politics: Germany declares war on Romania. Italy declares war on Germany.

29
Politics: Von Falkenhayn is sacked for failing at Verdun and is replaced by Field Marshal Paul von Hindenburg as Chief of German General staff. Von Ludendorff becomes Chief Quartermaster-General. Between them they control almost all Central Powers forces on the Eastern and Western Fronts.

30
Politics: Turkey declares war on Romania.

The Queen's Bays (2nd Dragoon Guards) moving up behind the Somme front.

September 1916
Stalemate in the fighting on the Eastern Front, in Galicia, and in Italy. Romania is attacked by the Central Powers and is overrun.

1
Politics: Bulgaria declares war on Romania.

2
Balkans: Bulgarian forces invade Romania along the Dobrudja frontier.

Great Britain: The first German airship shot down over Britain. During the remainder of the year an additional four Zeppelins are brought down over Britain.

3
Africa: Dar-es-Salaam the port and capital of German East Africa surrenders to British naval forces.

1916

Retreat from Gallipoli
JAN

German Verdun offensive starts
FEB

Unrestricted U-boat warfare begins again; Sussex torpedoed
MAR

Easter Rising in Ireland
APR

Crucial sea Battle of Jutland; German fleet returns to harbour for rest of war
MAY

Arab Revolt takes Mecca; US/Mex clash at Carr
J

The U-boat stranglehold—another merchantman is claimed.

Balkans: A combined army of Germans, Turks, and Bulgarians invades Romania, led by Mackensen, undermining any Romanian hopes of success;.

Western Front: Start of the Battle of Guillemont.

7
Balkans: The Bulgarians capture Tutrakan on the Danube taking 20,000 prisoners.

Eastern Front: Halicz burns and is taken by the Russians.

8
Western Front: Germany switches tactics from offense to defence in depth.

9
Balkans: Silistria on the Danube falls.

13
Italian Front: Italians defeat Austrians on the Carso.

14
Italian Front: Start of the Seventh Battle of the Isonzo.

15
Western Front: Battle of the Somme: Great British advance along a six-mile front on the Somme sees the capture of Flers, Courcelette, and other Germans positions. Success due in part to first use of British tanks at Flers-Courcelette.

19
Africa: Tabora in East Africa is occupied by Belgian troops under General Tombeur.

Somme offensive in west: 60,000 British casualties on first day
JUL

Romania joins war on Allied side
AUG

First use of tanks at Flers-Courcelette
SEP

French counteroffensive at Verdun
OCT

Lawrence of Arabia joins Arab army; end of Somme offensive
NOV

Romania beaten; President Wilson's peace note published
DEC

The first appearance of tanks in 15 September 1916, took the Germans by surprise.

Bottom: 9 August 1916. From left to right: Foch, Poincaré, the King, Joffre, Haig.

British troops returning to rest billets after capturing the village of Guillemont, during fighting on the Somme in July 1916.

20
Eastern Front: End of the Brusilov Offensive leaves the Austrian Army in shreds.

23
Western Front: Germany begins constructing the Hindenburg Line of defensive fortifications behind the German central and northern sectors.

25
Western Front: Battle of the Somme: The Battles of Morval and Thiepval Ridge continue the Allied advance.

26
Western Front: Combles and Thiepval captured by British and French.

27
Middle East: The massacre of Turkish troops in the village of Tafas south of the city of Damascus by Arab forces led by T. E. Lawrence when he gave his infamous order to 'take no prisoners'.

29
Balkans: Romanians begin retreat from Transylvania.

October 1916
The Allies again take the initative in France and resume the offensive in the Battle of the Somme.

1
Balkans: Austro-German attacks on Romania lead to enormous Romanian losses.

111

Retreat from Gallipoli
JAN

German Verdun offensive starts
FEB

Unrestricted U-boat warfare begins again; Sussex torpedoed
MAR

Easter Rising in Ireland
APR

Crucial sea Battle of Jutland; German fleet returns to harbour for rest of war
MAY

Arab Revolt takes Mecca; US/Mex clash at Carr
J

General Sir Beauvoir de Lisle addressing a battalion of the 29th division before one of the battles of the Somme.

Western Front: Battle of the Somme: British offensive – Battle of Ancre Heights, until 11 October; Battle of Transloy Ridges, until 20 October.

10

Italian Front: Eighth Battle of the Isonzo starts with the Battle of the Carso. The successful Italian attack wins ground and over 5,000 prisoners.

14

Balkans: Austro-German forces have pushed Romanians completely out of Transylvania except in the northeast corner.

15

War at sea: Germany resumes U-boat attacks under search and destroy rules.

21

Politics: The Austrian Premier Count Stürgkh is assassinated by Dr. F. Adler.

23

Eastern Front: Constanza falls to Austro-German forces.

24

Western Front: French recapture Douaumont Fort at Verdun. French forces recapture the strategic fortress of Douaumont. Verdun is saved.

29

War at sea: In the Aegean Greek volunteer transport Angeliki is torpedoed by a German submarine.

November 1916
The Allied attacks on the Western Front grind

Somme offensive in west: 60,000 British casualties on first day **JUL**

Romania joins war on Allied side **AUG**

First use of tanks at Flers-Courcelette **SEP**

French counteroffensive at Verdun **OCT**

Lawrence of Arabia joins Arab army; end of Somme offensive **NOV**

Romania beaten; President Wilson's peace note published **DEC**

The line of an evacuated German trench winds across the Somme valley which was devastated by the battles that raged there in summer and autumn 1916.

A British wiring party sets out to consolidate positions won from the Germans in the action at Morlay during the British advance in September 1916.

to an impasse. In central Europe Austro-Hungarian forces are closing in on Bucharest.

1

Italian Front: Start of the Ninth Battle of the Isonzo.

2

Western Front: Fort Vaux evacuated by the Germans.

5

Politics: Germany announces that Poland is to be established as an independent state – with German interests at heart.

7

United States: Democratic president Woodrow Wilson defeats Republican candidate Charles E. Hughes and is re-elected President of the

United States on a promise to keep the U.S. out of the war. Wilson's victory is narrow and uncertain until the Californian returns – 277 to 254 in the electoral college.

13

Western Front: Battle of the Ancre starts the fourth phase of the Battle of the Somme. The British advance along the Ancre river and capture the St Pierre Division and the field fortress of Beaumont Hamel taking almost 4,000 German prisoners.

18

Western Front: End of the Battle of the Somme. The offensive finally comes to an end. A total of 1.1 million British, French and German soldiers have been killed or wounded. The British lost 420,000 and the French almost 200,000 casualties. The Germans

113

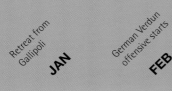

Retreat from Gallipoli **JAN**

German Verdun offensive starts **FEB**

Unrestricted U-boat warfare begins again; Sussex torpedoed **MAR**

Easter Rising in Ireland **APR**

Crucial sea Battle of Jutland; German fleet returns to harbour for rest of war **MAY**

Arab Revolt takes Mecca; US/Mex clash at Car **J**

Seaforth Highlanders during the battle of the Somme.

are estimated to have lost around 500,000 casualties.

19
Balkans: French and Serb forces capture Monastir in their joint advance. German and Bulgarian forces retreat toward Prilep.

21
Politics: Austro-Hungarian emperor Franz Josef dies aged 86 and succeeded by Kaiser Karl (Charles I) a liberal with a French wife.

War at sea: Britannic, the huge British hospital ship and sister ship to RMS Titanic, sunk by a mine or torpedo in Aegean Sea.

24
War at sea: British hospital ship Braemar Castle sinks after being torpedoed or mined in the Aegean.

23
War at sea: German warships bombard English coast.

28
Balkans: The Romanian government is transferred to Jassy.

Western Front: First German airplane raid on Britain. A German LVG C.IV seaplane raided London leaving ten injured. On its return flight, it develops engine trouble and is forced to crash land at Boulogne and its crew is captured.

28
Balkans: Bulgarian forces take and occupy Giurgevevo on the River Danube.

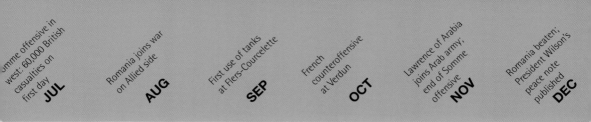

Somme offensive in west: 60,000 British casualties on first day **JUL**

Romania joins war on Allied side **AUG**

First use of tanks at Flers-Courcelette **SEP**

French counteroffensive at Verdun **OCT**

Lawrence of Arabia joins Arab army; end of Somme offensive **NOV**

Romania beaten; President Wilson's peace note published **DEC**

Men of the Wiltshire Regiment during the battle of the Somme.

Bottom: Germans captured at Thiepval, today the site of Lutyens' memorial to the missing.

29
General: Admiral Sir D. Beatty becomes commander in chief of the British Grand Fleet as Admiral Sir J. Jellicoe becomes First Sea Lord.

December 1916
Across Europe everyone is exhausted by the war. Germany experiences the 'Turnip Winter.' Because of the Allied blockade and poor planning, German soldiers and civilians alike have to subsist on little more than cattle feed for several months.

1
Balkans: 3,000 British, French, and Italian troops enter Athens after landing at Piraeus. They force surrender of Greek arms and munitions.

Tanks first appeared on the Somme in September 1916 — this one has just taken part in the action.

Politics: Political crisis in Britain as David Lloyd George resigns from the Government citing his frustration with the slow progress of the war.

2
Balkans: All Greek vessels are embargoed in Allied ports and Greece herself is blockaded by the Allies.

5
Politics: In Britain the political crisis deepens as Asquith resigns as Prime Minister.

6
Balkans: Bucharest, the capital of Romania is captured by Austro-German troops — effectively knocking Romania out of the war.

1917

Zimmerman telegram urges
German ambassador to
provoke war between
Mexico and the U.S.
JAN

U.S. breaks diplomatic
relations with
Germany
FEB

Russian Revolution
MAR

United States
declares war
on Germany
APR

Pershing given
command of AEF
MAY

British offensive
at Messines
J

The 39th siege battery of the Royal Garrison Artillery engaged in a bombardment during the Battle of the Somme.

7

Politics: In Britain David Lloyd George succeeds Asquith as Prime Minister.

9

Balkans: The Central Powers defeat Romania, gaining vital supplies.

Politics: In Britain a new War Cabinet is formed and three new ministries – of Shipping, Food, and Labour.

12

General: French General Robert Nivelle becomes Western Front commander-in-chief replacing General Joffre who becomes Technical War Advisor to the War Cabinet. The Air Board approves expansion of the RFC to 106 front-line squadrons and 95 reserve and training squadrons.

Politics: Germany issues a 'Peace Note' stating she was not responsible for the war but will agree to peace provided she keeps all territory gained. Any refusal will mean the Allies are responsible for further bloodshed. No specific terms are offered.

14

Balkans: The Allies give Greece a 24-hour ultimatum to withdraw their troops from Thessaly and cease aggression against the Allies.

15

Western Front: General Nivelle launches a massive French assault on German trenches at Verdun.

20

United States: Anxious to resolve the conflict as it is damaging the U.S. economy, President

Arab Revolt
takes Aqaba
JUL

Third Battle of Ypres
(Passchendaele)
AUG

Germans take Riga
in the east
SEP

German Caparetto
offensive on
Italian Front
OCT

October Revolution
in Russia brings Lenin
to power;
Battle of Cambrai
NOV

Armistice on the
Eastern Front;
Allies take
Jerusalem
DEC

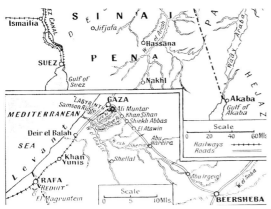

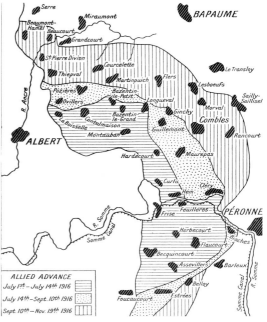

The Somme area, showing the three British advance stages between 1 July and 19 November 1916.

Bottom: Serbian troops advancing to attack Austro-German held Monastir. Serbians joined other Allied Salonika-based troops in retaking the city.

Wilson hands a Peace Note to all the belligerents asking them to state their peace terms and war objectives. He particularly offends the British by implying that their war aims are as immoral as Germany's.

18
Western Front: End of the Battle of Verdun – the longest battle of the war, ultimately defended by the French at great cost to both sides.

26
Politics: Germany replies to President's note and suggests a peace conference.

30
Politics: French government replies on behalf

Map of the area between Egypt and Palestine, scene of the British advance in 1916.

of Allies to President Wilson's peace note. They refuse to discuss peace till Germany agrees to restore lost liberties, pay reparation, and give guarantees not to infringe the independence of small nations – especially of Belgium.

1917

January 1917
The fighting continues as American attempts to broker a peace fail.

1
Politics: Turkey declares its independence of suzerainty of European powers.

War at sea: Cunard liner Ivernia is sunk in the Mediterranean: 153 reported missing.

1917

Zimmerman telegram urges German ambassador to provoke war between Mexico and the U.S. **JAN**

U.S. breaks diplomatic relations with Germany **FEB**

Russian Revolution **MAR**

United States declares war on Germany **APR**

Pershing given command of AEF **MAY**

British offensiv at Messines **J**

Field Marshal von Mackensen enters Bucharest after it fell to the Germans.

7

Eastern Front: Battle of the Aa in Lithuania. Limited russian attack as the Twelfth Amry unexpectedly attacked German positions along a 30 mile front.

9

Mesopotamia: British forces attack Khadairi Bend.

War at sea: In the Mediterranean HMS Cornwallis is sunk by enemy submarine: 13 lost.

10

Politics: Allies extensively state their peace objectives in response to U.S. President Woodrow Wilson's peace note. They agree to a League of Nations but strongly refute that they bear any resemblence to the enemy's behaviour, motives and objectives.

16

Politics: German Foreign Minister Zimmerman sends a telegram from Berlin to the German ambassador in Mexico urging him to do whatever he can to provoke war between Mexico and the U.S. In return Mexico will get the return of southwestern U.S. British intelligence intercepts the transmission and starts decoding it.

17

United States: The United States pays Denmark $25 million for the Virgin Islands.

20

Balkans: The Romanians establish an effective front along the Sereth River.

22

United States: In Washington D.C. President Wilson calls for 'peace without victory.'

Arab Revolt takes Aqaba
JUL

Third Battle of Ypres (Passchendaele)
AUG

Germans take Riga in the east
SEP

German Caparetto offensive on Italian Front
OCT

October Revolution in Russia brings Lenin to power; Battle of Cambrai
NOV

Armistice on the Eastern Front; Allies take Jerusalem
DEC

The Battle of the Ancre, 11-21 November 1916.

Bottom: A British gun emplacement near Mametz. The German wicker shell-cases show that the position was recently taken. In the background a field battery is moving up to a new postion.

General Robert Nivelle won fame in command at Verdun and succeeded Joffre as commander-in-chief in December 1916.

Wilson has become convinced that both sides must cease fighting immediately and talk instead.

23

War at sea: Action off Schouwen Bank, Harwich Force destroyer Simoom is torpedoed by S.50 between Maas and north Hinder LVs.

25

United States: The Danish West Indies is sold to the United States for $25 million.

28

United States: The United States ends the search for Pancho Villa.

31

War at sea: In Berlin Germany announces unrestricted submarine warfare in the war zone as of 1 February. This way Germany attempts to starve Britain into submission before the U.S. becomes willing and able to intervene. Warns neutrals that all ships entering the zone will be sunk without warning.

February 1917

Austria-Hungary opens secret peace negotiations with France, while in Russia there is general unrest. Germany tries to break Britain and win a quick victory using submarine warfare.

3

United States: Due in part to continued German naval action the U.S. severs

119

1917

Zimmerman telegram urges German ambassador to provoke war between Mexico and the U.S.
JAN

U.S. breaks diplomatic relations with Germany
FEB

Russian Revolution
MAR

United States declares war on Germany
APR

Pershing given command of AEF
MAY

British offensive at Messines
J

With the ruins of the village of Contalmaison in the distance, two bands of men pass each other: a working party carrying picks and Australian machine-gunners leaving the trenches.

diplomatic relations with Germany and demands the return of 72 American sailors on board the British steamer Yarrowdale, captured by a German raider. The following day the German ambassador Count Von Bernstorff is handed his passports and the U.S. ambassador in Berlin is recalled.

3
War at sea: American steamer Housatonic sunk by U-boat near the Scilly Islands off the southwest coast of England.

5
United States: British General Staff estimates that no more than 250,000 American soldiers could be in Europe even after a year — an error as will be seen.
The constitution of Mexico is adopted.

7
War at sea: SS California of the Anchor liner is sunk without warning off the Irish coast by a submarine: 46 reported lost, 160 survivors.

9
Western Front: Orders given for Operation 'Alberich,' where German troops withdraw 25 miles to the Hindenburg Line.

13
War at sea: White Star liner Afric is sunk by a German submarine.

17
Western Front: British troops on the Ancre capture German positions.

21
Western Front: Operation 'Alberich' starts.

Arab Revolt
takes Aqaba
JUL

Third Battle of Ypres
(Passchendaele)
AUG

Germans take Riga
in the east
SEP

German Caporetto
offensive on
Italian Front
OCT

October Revolution
in Russia brings Lenin
to power;
Battle of Cambrai
NOV

Armistice on the
Eastern Front;
Allies take
Jerusalem
DEC

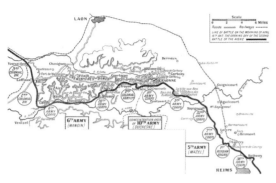

District of the Chemin des Dames and the river Aisne where Nivelle conducted his French offensive.

Bottom: Guarded by a sentry a wrecked British R.E.8 lies beside a road near Boesinghe. The pilot escaped but the undercarriage was badly damaged and the propeller smashed.

German forces begin withdrawal to strong positions on the Hindenburg Line.

The Fricourt road in the Somme area as one of the few thoroughfares was often congested with men and machines.

Mesopotamia: Kut-el-Amara is evacuated by the Turks and they retreat toward Baghdad. Occupied by the British.

23

Western Front: No. 100 Sqn arrives in France as the first night bomber squadron. It is equipped with FE2b aircraft.

24

United States: U.S. ambassador to the U.K. Walter H. Page is handed Zimmermann Telegram by Britain. It details the German proposal of an alliance with Mexico against the U.S. if Mexico declares war on the U.S.

Western Front: The Germans are evacuate the villages of Pys, Petit Miraumont, Warlencourt and Serre.

25

War at sea: Cunard liner SS Laconia, torpedoed and sunk off the Irish coast with losses including four Americans.

26

United States: President Woodrow Wilson requests permission from Congress to arm U.S. merchantmen. The Senate, led by La Follette of Wisconsin, refuse to grant Wilson power to wage an undeclared naval war.

28

United States: U.S. government makes public the Zimmermann Telegram from Germany to Mexico proposing an alliance, and offering as

121

1917

Zimmerman telegram urges German ambassador to provoke war between Mexico and the U.S.
JAN

U.S. breaks diplomatic relations with Germany
FEB

Russian Revolution
MAR

United States declares war on Germany
APR

Pershing given command of AEF
MAY

British offensive at Messines
JU

In 1917 'Blimps' (non-rigid airships) could fly for 50 hours at speeds up to 50mph. The gondola is an adapted fuselage from a 90 horse power B.E. plane.

a reward the return of Mexico's lost territories in Texas, New Mexico, and Arizona.

March 1917

The February Revolution (so-called because it takes place in February according to the Russian Julian calendar) convulses Russia and overthrows the Czarist regime, damaging the willpower and ability of the Russian armed forces. Elsewhere the British fail in Palestine but prevail in Messopotamia.

1
United States: Details of the Zimmermann telegram are published in the U.S. press. An angry Congress debates the Armed Ship Bill.

3
United States: Mexico denies having received an offer from Germany suggesting an alliance.

Western Front: British advance on Bapaume.

4
United States: The U.S. Senate adjourns without passing Armed Ship Bill as requested by the President.

6
War at sea: Austria publicly stands by Germany's U-boat policy of ruthless warfare.

7
United States: President Wilson decides to arm U.S. ships despite Congress' refusal to agree.

9
Russian Revolution: Food riots in Petrograd, formerly St. Petersburg, Russia.

Arab Revolt
takes Aqaba
JUL

Third Battle of Ypres
(Passchendaele)
AUG

Germans take Riga
in the east
SEP

German Caparetto
offensive on
Italian Front
OCT

October Revolution
in Russia brings Lenin
to power;
Battle of Cambrai
NOV

Armistice on the
Eastern Front;
Allies take
Jerusalem
DEC

From left to right: Sir Herbert Plumer (c-in-c Second Army), Sir Edmund Allenby (c-in-c Third Army) and Sir Henry Horne (c-in-c First Army), at Camblain Chatelain in February 1917.

Bottom: Romanian machine-gunners in a snow-covered Moldavian wood in February 1917.

10
Russian Revolution: Russian Czar suspends sittings of the Duma — the Russian parliament.

11
Balkans: Battle of Lake Prespa. The Allies start the Spring Campaign in Macedonia by attacking from Salonika to the north and northwest of Mostar.

Mesopotamia: Led by General Maude British forces capture Baghdad after three days of fighting.

Aerial view of the Héninel section of the Hindenburg Line clearly shows the strength of the trench systems.

12
United States: U.S. President Woodrow Wilson announces the arming of U.S. merchantmen by executive order after failing to win approval from Congress.

13
Russian Revolution: Moscow in hands of revolutionaries.

14
Politics: China breaks diplomatic relations with Germany.

War at sea: American steamer Algonquin torpedoed without warning.

15
Russian Revolution: Nicholas II abdicates on this day (2 March in Julian calendar).

123

1917

Zimmerman telegram urges German ambassador to provoke war between Mexico and the U.S.
JAN

U.S. breaks diplomatic relations with Germany
FEB

Russian Revolution
MAR

United States declares war on Germany
APR

Pershing given command of AEF
MAY

British offensive at Messines
JU

Mesopotamian Front: British troops advance up the Tigris in spring 1917.

16
Russian Revolution: A provisional government is formed in Russia. Prince Lvoff heads the new cabinet. General Mikhail Alexeev becomes commander in chief.

17
Politics: In France the government of Aristide Briand falls.

Western Front: Bapaume falls to British. Roye and Lassigny are occupied by the French.

18
War at sea: U.S. ships City of Memphis, Illinois, and Vigilancia, sunk by German submarines.

Western Front: Peronne, Chaulnes, Nesle and Noyon evacuated by Germans, who retire on an 85-mile front.

19
War at sea: In the Mediterranean the French battleship Danton is torpedoed: 296 lost.

20
Politics: In France Alexander Ribot becomes French premier, succeeding Briand.

United States: U.S. President Woodrow Wilson's war cabinet votes unanimously in favor of declaring war on Germany.

21
War at sea: U.S. ship Healdton bound from Philadelphia to Rotterdam, is sunk without warning: 21 men lost.

25
Mesopotamia: Battle of Jebel Hamrin starts with an Anglo-Russian move to encircle 15,000 Turkish soldiers. The attempt failed.

Arab Revolt takes Aqaba **JUL**

Third Battle of Ypres (Passchendaele) **AUG**

Germans take Riga in the east **SEP**

German Caparetto offensive on Italian Front **OCT**

October Revolution in Russia brings Lenin to power; Battle of Cambrai **NOV**

Armistice on the Eastern Front; Allies take Jerusalem **DEC**

Demonstration in Nevsky Prospect, Petrograd, after the February Revolution of 1917. The banner reads 'Liberty, Equality, Fraternity'.

Bottom: The 6in howitzer gave the British artillery superiority in Mesopotamia once the problems of climate and terrain were overcome by Sir Stanley Maude.

The Tigris between Amara and Baghdad.

26

Middle East: In Palestine the First Battle of Gaza begins. British cavalry troops retreat after 17,000 Turks block their advance.

Western Front: British start to advance on Cambrai.

29

Middle East: In Palestine British forces defeat 20,000 Turks.

United States: U.S. War College Division issues report on possible U.S. involvement in the war. States they would need a large trained force of between 500,000 and 1,000,000 men and (optimistically) estimate that at least ten months are needed to ship a force of 500,000 to Europe after recruiting and training. This puts earliest possible U.S. involvement to mid- to late-1918. They repeat that it is ridiculous to send an untrained American army overseas. President Wilson publicly calls for a national army to be 'raised and maintained exclusively by selective draft.'

31

Politics: The Danish West Indies become the Virgin Islands when Denmark transfers control over the islands to the U.S. after the purchase of the islands on 25 January for $25 million.

United States: Two British ships, Crispin and Snowdon Range, are torpedoed by U-boats: American passengers are killed.

1917

Zimmerman telegram urges German ambassador to provoke war between Mexico and the U.S.
JAN

U.S. breaks diplomatic relations with Germany
FEB

Russian Revolution
MAR

United States declares war on Germany
APR

Pershing given command of AEF
MAY

British offensive at Messines
J

Sir Stanley Maude entering Baghdad at the head of his troops after a three month campaign against the Turks. 11 March 1917.

April 1917

In April the German submarine campaign exacts the heaviest damage of the war: 881,027 gross tons, 500,000 of which are British. In the skies the first week became known as 'Bloody April.' The RFC lost 75 aircraft in action and the average life expectancy of a pilot in France was two months. By the end of the month the RFC had lost a total of 150 aircraft and 316 aircrew, the French and Belgians 200 aircraft, and the Germans 370. Between April and August mutinies began to rumble in the French armies. The United States moves onto a war footing.

Tsar Nicholas under guard at Tsarskoe Selo in the palace grounds. After the Tsar abduction on 15 March 1917, he was arrested and kept in the imperial palace at Tsarskoe Selo before being moved to Tobolsk in August.

Arab Revolt takes Aqaba
JUL

Third Battle of Ypres (Passchendaele)
AUG

Germans take Riga in the east
SEP

German Caparetto offensive on Italian Front
OCT

October Revolution in Russia brings Lenin to power; Battle of Cambrai
NOV

Armistice on the Eastern Front; Allies take Jerusalem
DEC

Curious as to how well the new British weapon manoeuvres, this captured tank is being tested for its climbing capability. It has already been painted in German livery.

Limbers and lorries moving up a sunken road towards the front. German prisoners are helping to lay wounded men beside the road.

127

Zimmerman telegram urges German ambassador to provoke war between Mexico and the U.S. **JAN**

U.S. breaks diplomatic relations with Germany **FEB**

Russian Revolution **MAR**

United States declares war on Germany **APR**

Pershing given command of AEF **MAY**

British offensive at Messines **JI**

Some of the first mobilized American troops marching through the streets of New York in April 1917.

1

War at sea: American armed ship, Aztec is sunk in the submarine zone.

2

United States: President Woodrow Wilson addresses Congress at 8:32pm. He cites: the damaging U-boat activity, the threat proposed by the Zimmerman telegram, the British need help, and – 'The world must be made safe for democracy.' He asks Congress for a declaration of war on Germany.

4

United States: Wilson's resolution is passed by by the Senate 82-6.

5

War at sea: American steamer Missourian is sunk in the Mediterranean by a German submarine.

6

United States: The United States declares war on Germany after being passed by the House 373-50 and signed by President Wilson. U.S. mobilization begins. The U.S. Navy and Marine Corps possessed 54 aircraft, 48 officers and 239 enlisted men. The U.S. Army Aviation Section had less than 300 aircraft, none of them combat types, and only 35 qualified pilots. General John 'Black Jack' Pershing is chosen to command the American Expeditionary Force.

7

Politics: Cuba and Panama declare war against Germany.

8

Politics: Austria-Hungary breaks diplomatic relations with the United States.

Arab Revolt
takes Aqaba
JUL

Third Battle of Ypres
(Passchendaele)
AUG

Germans take Riga
in the east
SEP

German Caparetto
offensive on
Italian Front
OCT

October Revolution
in Russia brings Lenin
to power;
Battle of Cambrai
NOV

Armistice on the
Eastern Front;
Allies take
Jerusalem
DEC

German submariners rescue some of the crew of a merchant vessel they sunk only minutes before.

Bottom: Infantry pass beside a captured communication trench; a battery of 18-pounder field guns is in action; in the far distance a squadron of cavalry moves up.

Russian Revolution: Lenin and other Bolshevik revolutionaries start their journey back to Russia.

9

Politics: Brazil severs diplomatic relations with Germany.

Politics: Bolivia severs diplomatic relations with Germany.

Western Front: Start of the Nivelle Offensive starts with a British attack around Arras and ultimately ends in failure. The Arras offensive takes place on a 12-mile front from Hénin-sur-Cojeul to Givenchy-en-Gohelle. Battle of Vimy Ridge. Capture of Vimy Ridge and the surrounding area, Givenchy, Bailleul

Struck by a floating mine, this merchant ship was an easy target, and in all probability sunk within minutes.

and positions about Lens by Canadian troops: they take 6,000 prisoners.

14

United States: U.S. George Creel's Committee for Public Information is set up to help sway U.S. public opinion on the side of the war.

16

Russian Revolution: Lenin arrives in Russia at Petrograd (St Petersburg) having been transported by the Germans.

Western Front: Start of the French part of the Nivelle Offensive — aka Second Battle of the Aisne — against German positions on the Chemin des Dames ridge. This plan of assault fails, destroying French morale. Casualties reach 150,000 by May 5 and will spark off mutinies in the French army. Nivelle is dismissed for his incompetence.

Zimmerman telegram urges German ambassador to provoke war between Mexico and the U.S.
JAN

U.S. breaks diplomatic relations with Germany
FEB

Russian Revolution
MAR

United States declares war on Germany
APR

Pershing given command of AEF
MAY

British offensive at Messines

On Easter Day, 9 April 1917 where others had failed, the Canadians finally managed to capture Vimy Ridge.

17
Western Front: French tanks used for the first time in battle.

19
Middle East: Second Battle of Gaza. Attempt by British forces to breach the Turkish defensive line.

20
Politics: Turkey breaks diplomatic relations with United States.

23
Mesopotamia: British forces occupy Samarrah, some 60 miles north of Baghdad and take 937 prisoners.

United States: The U.S. breaks diplomatic relations with Turkey.

Western Front: Second phase of the Battle of Arras begins as the British attack north and south of the River Scarpe.

27
Politics: Guatemala breaks diplomatic relations with Germany.

War at sea: Submarine attacks force the Allies to divert shipping from the Suez Canal.

28
United States: U.S. Congress passes the Army Bill allowing conscription of American citizens.

29
Western Front: Serious outbreak of mutiny in the French Army – lasts until mid-June. They defend their lines but refuse to mount new assaults.

Arab Revolt takes Aqaba
JUL

Third Battle of Ypres (Passchendaele)
AUG

Germans take Riga in the east
SEP

German Caparetto offensive on Italian Front
OCT

October Revolution in Russia brings Lenin to power; Battle of Cambrai
NOV

Armistice on the Eastern Front; Allies take Jerusalem
DEC

Canadian troops resting after capturing a German battery of high velocity guns. However, this gun was put out of action before the defenders fled.

Tank stuck in a muddy ditch during Arras offensive, April 1917.

Bottom: French tanks were first used in combat in 1917.

31
War at sea: Germany announces that all vessels in the war zone around British Isles are viable targets for sinking.

May 1917
The French Army is demoralized and exhausted. Mutiny seriously threatens their war efforts. Between May and October the Italians fight the Tenth, Eleventh and Twelfth Battles of the Isonzo. All end in Italian failure. In America due to the Selective Service Act 2,800,000 U.S. citizens are drafted. 42 Divisions are sent to France, at this stage a total of 2,084,000 men.

1
United States: U.S. Army Expansion Act inflates the armed forces from 200,000 to 4,791,172. 32 new cantonments and camps are to be built, including Camp Kearny and Camp Fremont in California each designed to take 40,000 soldiers at a cost of $262m.

3
Western Front: Major British attack along a 12-mile front east of Arras, breaking through the Hindenburg switch at Quéant and taking Fresnoy.

4
War at sea: In the Mediterranean British transport ship Arcadian is torpedoed: 277 lost. Another British transport also torpedoed there: Transylvania with 413 lost.

131

1917

Zimmerman telegram urges German ambassador to provoke war between Mexico and the U.S.
JAN

U.S. breaks diplomatic relations with Germany
FEB

Russian Revolution
MAR

United States declares war on Germany
APR

Pershing given command of AEF
MAY

British offensive at Messines
J

The crew escape the fires on the lower deck during the last moments of the French liner Sontay, sunk by a torpedo in the Mediterranean on 16 April 1917.

5
Western Front: French force supported by British troops take the crest of Craonne ridge. At Chemin des Dames they capture 6,000 German prisoners.

8
Politics: Liberia breaks off diplomatic relations with Germany.

10
War at sea: Britain introduces the convoy system to protect shipping from enemy submarine activity.

11
Russian Revolution: Russian Council of Workmen's and Soldiers' Delegates demands a peace conference.

14
Italian Front: Start of the Tenth Battle of the Isonzo.

15
War at sea: In the Adriatic the Battle of the Otranto Straits starts when Austro-Hungarian cruisers and destroyers attack the Allied Otranto Barrage. This is the largest surface action of the naval war in the Mediterranean.

Western Front: General Pétain succeeds General Nivelle as Commander-in-Chief of the French Western Front armies. General Foch is appointed Chief of Staff. Pétain becomes French C-in-C. Two days later Pétain announces a temporary French switch from offense to defense.

Arab Revolt takes Aqaba

JUL

Third Battle of Ypres (Passchendaele)

AUG

Germans take Riga in the east

SEP

German Caparetto offensive on Italian Front

OCT

October Revolution in Russia brings Lenin to power; Battle of Cambrai

NOV

Armistice on the Eastern Front; Allies take Jerusalem

DEC

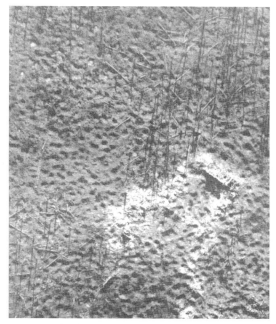

Well fortified German gun emplacement in Farbus Wood, (beyond Vimy Ridge) being checked over by two Canadian soldiers after its capture on 9 April 1917.

Bottom: With its load of shells on the side of the road, Canadian troops manhandle a truck from a shellhole near Vimy.

Oppy wood, village and chateau were obliterated by British bombing — but remained in German hands. May 1917.

16

United States: U.S. Sedition Act, one of a number of pieces of legislation that curtailed civil liberties in order to enforce conformity to the war effort.

Western Front: Bullecourt captured by British in the Battle of Arras.

17

Politics: Honduras breaks diplomatic relations with Germany.

18

United States: Selective Service Act (Conscription bill) is signed by President Wilson. The act gave the President the power to draft soldiers. Nearly ten million men are listed and a lottery chooses the first 687,000 to serve. Eventually 3,000,000 men serve as draftees in the war.

19

Politics: Nicaragua severs diplomatic relations with Germany.

22

Italian Front: Italians advance on the Carso.

23

Italian Front: Great Italian advance from Kostanjevica to the sea.

24

War at sea: Japanese destroyers enter the Mediterranean.

1917

Zimmerman telegram urges German ambassador to provoke war between Mexico and the U.S.
JAN

U.S. breaks diplomatic relations with Germany
FEB

Russian Revolution
MAR

United States declares war on Germany
APR

Pershing given command of AEF
MAY

British offensive at Messines
J

Sir Jacob van Deventer took over from General Smuts in May 1917 and conquered German East Africa.

26
United States: First U.S. troops arrive in France.

War at sea: French Minister of Marine announces that German submarines have sunk 2,400,000 tons of shipping in the first four months of the year.

28
United States: General Pershing and his staff leave New York harbor for France aboard the Baltic.

30
Politics: The Lithuanian National Council is instituted in an attempt to form a German puppet state.

June 1917
The responsibility for attack on the Western Front goes to the BEF as French forces are too exhausted for constant assaults. Greece enters the war.

2
Politics: Brazil revokes her neutrality and seizes all German ships within her territorial waters.

3
Italian Front: Austria launches a great counter-offensive on San Marco, east of Gorizia. Leads to very heavy fighting as the Italians are forced back.

Politics: Albania proclaims her independence under Italian protection.

Arab Revolt
takes Aqaba
JUL

Third Battle of Ypres
(Passchendaele)
AUG

Germans take Riga
in the east
SEP

German Caporetto
offensive on
Italian Front
OCT

October Revolution
in Russia brings Lenin
to power;
Battle of Cambrai
NOV

Armistice on the
Eastern Front;
Allies take
Jerusalem
DEC

Anti-aircraft station manned by men from the Royal Naval Air Service, situated in the grounds of the Metropolitan Water Board, near Mount Pleasant, London

Above: Area of operations around Messines in June 1917.

The course of the Isonzo river marked the chief battle ground on the Italian front in 1917.

4

Russian Revolution: General Alexei Brusilov is appointed commander in chief of the Russian Army by the Provisional Government.

5

United States: Registration day for new draft army in United States.

7

United States: U.S. General Staff issues plan to ship American forces at a rate of 120,000 per month beginning in August; in fact, this rate of dispatch is not realized until April 1918

General John J. Pershing, newly selected commander of the American Expeditionary Forces, arrives in England with his staff en route to France.

Western Front: Battle of Messines. British launch attack on Messines-Wytschaete ridge by exploding 19 large mines ; they capture capture the position.

11

Politics: King Constantine of Greece abdicates his throne in favor of his second son, Alexander.

13

Western Front: Germany launches the first heavy bomber raid against London. 18 Gotha aircraft kill 162 people and injure over 400. The RFC fails to shoot any of the raiders down.

14

United States: President Wilson, in his Flag Day Address, declares that the initial American Expeditionary Force will be

135

1917

Zimmerman telegram urges
German ambassador to
provoke war between
Mexico and the U.S.
JAN

U.S. breaks diplomatic
relations with
Germany
FEB

Russian Revolution
MAR

United States
declares war
on Germany
APR

Pershing given
command of AEF
MAY

British offensive
at Messines
JU

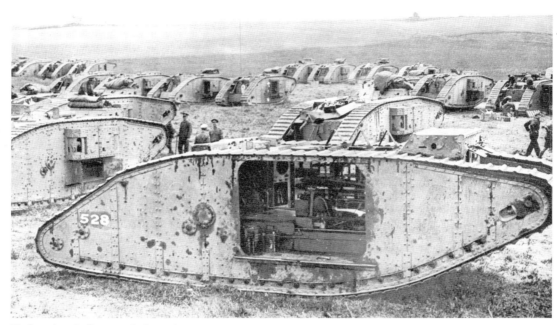

Tank park at Rollencourt in June 1917.

followed by more soldiers as quickly as possible, and that these soldiers will not be held in the US for training.

15
United States: U.S. Espionage Act passed – suspending normal constitutional freedoms for American citizens.

16
Russian Revolution: In Petrograd the first All-Russian Congress of Soviets is held.

20
United States: U.S. starts the first of five Liberty Loan drives: raises $23 billion of $32 billion cost of war: the rest is raised from new taxation.

25
United States: U.S. 1st Division troops began landing in France, they are the first American fighting contingent.

28 U.S. Bernard Baruch's War Industries Board centralizes the nation's economic output.

29
Politics: Greece breaks off diplomatic relations with Germany and Austria-Hungary and declares war on side of the Allies.

July 1917
The final Russian Offensive on the Eastern front fails.

1
Eastern Front: Russia begins an initially successful offensive in Galicia under the personal control of Kerensky, Russian Minister of War. Heavy fighting leaves many Russians dead but they take 12,000 prisoners. The

Arab Revolt
takes Aqaba
JUL

Third Battle of Ypres
(Passchendaele)
AUG

Germans take Riga
in the east
SEP

German Caparetto
offensive on
Italian Front
OCT

October Revolution
in Russia brings Lenin
to power;
Battle of Cambrai
NOV

Armistice on the
Eastern Front;
Allies take
Jerusalem
DEC

General Pershing arriving at Euston station, 8 June 1917. From left to right: Pershing, Walter Hines Page, Admiral Sims and Lord Derby.

Italian troops near Val D'Assa.

assault ends after a German counter offensive with a 150 mile retreat by the Russians on 23 July.

General John Pershing disembarking at Boulogne, France, on 13 June 1917.

people and injuring 193. 108 sorties were launched in defence, and one Gotha was shot down, and three others suffered severe damage. Two defending aircraft were also shot down.

2

United States: Pershing revises his estimate of the number of fighting men he needs: makes first request for an army of 1,000,000 men.

6

Politics: Canadian House of Commons passes the Compulsory Military Service Bill.

7

Politics: In the German Reichstag a peace resolution is tabled: passed on the 19th.

Western Front: 22 Gothas launch a second daylight air attack on London, killing 57

9

War at sea: British dreadnought Vanguard blows up in Scapa Flow while at anchor.

11

United States: On reflection Pershing says that 1,000,000 men is only the initial size and that his army will require upwards of 3,000,000.

14

Politics: German Imperial Chancellor Herr von Bethmann Hollweg resigns and is replaced by Dr Michaelis.

1917

Zimmerman telegram urges German ambassador to provoke war between Mexico and the U.S.
JAN

U.S. breaks diplomatic relations with Germany
FEB

Russian Revolution
MAR

United States declares war on Germany
APR

Pershing given command of AEF
MAY

British offensive at Messines
JU

Greece joins the war after the fall of the monarchy, June 1917.

16

Eastern Front: Start of retreat of Russians on a front of 155 miles.

Middle East: T. E. Lawrence and Arab forces take Aqaba from the Turks by mounting a suprise attack after crossing the Nefu dessert.

17

Politics: King George V changes the royal family names from Hanover to Windsor and Battemgerg to Mountbatten.

19

Politics: Germany's parliament, the Reichstag, passes a resolution calling for a negotiated peace with the Allies. General Ludendorff sets up a Patriotic Instruction Programme to counter such sentiments and bolster German morale.

20

Russian Revolution: Alexander Kerensky becomes Russian premier, succeeding Lvoff.

United States: Drawing of draft number for American conscript army begins.

25

Politics: Sir Thomas Whyte introduces the first income tax in Canada as a 'temporary' measure. The lowest bracket is 4 percent and highest is 25 percent.

31

Western Front: Third Battle of Ypres – better known as Passchendaele – starts with a huge artillery barrage as the precusor for a major British-French attack on a 15-mile front in Flanders. The initial thrust takes 12 villages and 5,000 prisoners. Third Ypres lasts until mid-November.

Arab Revolt takes Aqaba
JUL

Third Battle of Ypres (Passchendaele)
AUG

Germans take Riga in the east
SEP

German Caparetto offensive on Italian Front
OCT

October Revolution in Russia brings Lenin to power; Battle of Cambrai
NOV

Armistice on the Eastern Front; Allies take Jerusalem
DEC

A loyal Russian soldier threatens two would-be deserters with his rifle butt in an attempt to restore order to the ranks.
Bottom: Aleksandr Kerenski (centre), Russian premier after the Bolshevik revolution, watches the funeral of Cossacks killed during the July rising.

Arabia and the Red Sea, showing the area of the campaigns by Arabs to free themselves from the Turks.

31
War at sea: At Wilhelmshaven the German High Seas Fleet, bored and frustrated at their inaction since 1916, are ready for mutiny. Trouble started on the dreadnought Prinz Regent Luitpold but is quickly stopped.

August 1917
The numbers of dead and wounded mount up as the battles for Ypres and Verdun are fought. China enters the war on the side of the Allies.

1
Politics: Pope Benedict XV makes plea for peace on the basis of no annexation, no indemnity influences and impresses President Wilson.

2
War at sea: First ever landing by an aircraft on a ship under way when a Sopwith Pup landed on the deck of the converted light cruiser HMS Furious. Five days later the pilot was killed attempting the same maneuver.

7
Politics: Liberia declares war against Germany.

8
Politics: Canadian Conscription Bill passes its third reading in Senate. The Compulsory Military Service Bill ends the promise of no conscription made by Prime Minister Borden.

14
Politics: China declares war on Germany and Austria-Hungary.

1917

Zimmerman telegram urges German ambassador to provoke war between Mexico and the U.S.
JAN

U.S. breaks diplomatic relations with Germany
FEB

Russian Revolution
MAR

United States declares war on Germany
APR

Pershing given command of AEF
MAY

British offensiv at Messines
J

Austrian officers at battle HQ after the capture of the Austro-German fortress of Czernowitz in August 1917 — the 15th and last time the town changed hands during the war.

15

Western Front: Big British assault on a wide front northwest of Lens. Canadian troops capture Hill 70, dominating Lens. Five German counter-attacks are successfully repulsed.

15

War at sea: British Q-ships trawling smacks Nelson and Ethel & Millie are sunk by UC63.

16

Western Front: Allies attack on a nine-mile front between Lens and the Menin Road and crossing the Steenbeek River. They advance half a mile and take Langemarck.

19

Italian Front: Start of the Eleventh Battle of the Isonzo when the Italians cross the river and take Austrian positions. They attack on a 30-mile front between Carso and the sea. They push forward 25 miles and take 7,500 Austrain prisoners.

20

Western Front: Third Battle of Verdun starts as the French advance 1.25 miles as they assault an 11-mile front.

26

Italian Front: On the Southern Front almost the entire Bainsizza Plateau is held by Italians.

28

Western Front: At Verdun the French have resumed all the ground they have lost since the great German attack in February 1916.

Arab Revolt takes Aqaba
JUL

Third Battle of Ypres (Passchendaele)
AUG

Germans take Riga in the east
SEP

German Caparetto offensive on Italian Front
OCT

October Revolution in Russia brings Lenin to power; Battle of Cambrai
NOV

Armistice on the Eastern Front; Allies take Jerusalem
DEC

Unarmed workers in Petrograd being mown down by machine-gun fire during the abortive workers rising, 'The July Days', of 1917.

Bottom: British gunners try to pull an 18-pounder field-gun stuck in the thick mud near Zillebeke, during the British offensive in Flanders in 1917.

29
Politics: Pope Benedict's peace plea is finally rejected by President Wilson.

September 1917
The Russian Army is beaten into submission as the Germans inexorably advance toward Russia. Political crisis erupts in Russia as the republic is declared. The fighting at Ypres resumes in intensity.

1
Eastern Front: Germany takes the northernmost end of the Russian front in the Riga offensive. Captures Riga by using new tactics based on lightning assault.

American troops marching down Piccadilly, London, 14 August 1917.

Western Front: Pershing establishes his general headquarters at Chaumont.

2
Western Front: Start of numerous German air-raids on London and south-east England that last all month.

3
Eastern Front: Riga captured by Germans as the Russians are finally forced to evacuate the city blowing up bridges and forts as they go. The Germans claim to take many thousands of prisoners.

10
Russian Revolution: Kerensky becomes dictator of Russia.

1917

Zimmerman telegram urges
German ambassador to
provoke war between
Mexico and the U.S.
JAN

U.S. breaks diplomatic
relations with
Germany
FEB

Russian Revolution
MAR

United States
declares war
on Germany
APR

Pershing given
command of AEF
MAY

British offensive
at Messines
JU

An Australian Lewis gun team and a trench mortar enjoying a period of comparative quiet during the third battle of Ypres.

14
Politics: Paul Painleve becomes French premier, succeeding Ribot.

15
Russian Revolution: A Provisional Council of five proclaim Russia a republic led by Kerensky and a new war cabinet is formed.

20
Politics: Costa Rica breaks with Germany.

21
United States: General Tasker H. Bliss named Chief of Staff of the United States Army.

26
Western Front: East of Ypres the positions of Zonnebeke, Polygon Wood, and Tower Hamlets are taken by British.

29
Mesopotamia: Turkish Mesopotamian army, under Ahmed Bey, is captured by British.

October 1917
The Battle for Ypres still continues. The final battle of the Isonzo sees the Italian fighting spirit broken as the Austro-German forces overwhelm their lines.

3
United States: U.S. War Revenue Act authorizes graduated income tax.

6
Politics: Peru breaks off diplomatic relations with Germany.

7
Politics: Uruguay breaks off diplomatic relations with Germany.

Arab Revolt takes Aqaba
JUL

Third Battle of Ypres (Passchendaele)
AUG

Germans take Riga in the east
SEP

German Caparetto offensive on Italian Front
OCT

October Revolution in Russia brings Lenin to power; Battle of Cambrai
NOV

Armistice on the Eastern Front; Allies take Jerusalem
DEC

During the night of 4 September 1917 a German bomb dropped on the Embankment, London, chipped and damaged Cleopatra's Needle and Sphinxes.

Durham Light Infantry signallers in the line near Veldhoek in September 1917. They are equipped with a telescope and Morse signalling apparatus.

9

Africa: In East Africa Belgian troops occupy the German HQ of Mahenge.

Middle East: The Sultan of Egypt Hussein Kamel dies and is succeeded by his youngest brother Ahmed Fuad.

Western Front: Third phase of the Third Battle of Ypres. Poelcapelle and other German positions captured in Franco-British attack.

12

Politics: Sir Robert Borden wins Canadian election with a coalition government and is returned for another term in office.

Western Front: British Offensive at Passchendaele.

15

Western Front: At Vincennes outside Paris, Dutch dancer Mata Hari is executed by firing squad accused of spying for Germany.

17

War at sea: American transport Antilles, westbound from France, sunk by submarine: 67 lost.
Scandinavian Convoys. German attack on convoy by minelaying cruisers Brummer and Bremse. Destroyers Strongbow and Mary Rose sunk by gunfire 75 miles east of Lerwick. 9 of 12 merchant ships sunk.

19

Great Britain: The 'Silent Raid.' Eleven Zeppelins carry out the last airship raid over Britain. All five airships were lost – the biggest disaster suffered by the German

1917

Zimmerman telegram urges German ambassador to provoke war between Mexico and the U.S. **JAN**

U.S. breaks diplomatic relations with Germany **FEB**

Russian Revolution **MAR**

United States declares war on Germany **APR**

Pershing given command of AEF **MAY**

British offensive at Messines **JU**

Canadian premier Sir Robert Borden visiting the front to inspect members of the Canadian battalion commanded by his cousin.

Naval Airship Service. The raid was so called because the Zeppelins flew so high during the attack that the gun and searchlight emplacements were ordered to remain covered so as not to give away their locations.

23
Western Front: American troops in France fire their first shots in trench warfare. 1st Division of AEF on Swiss border.
French advance northeast of Soissons.

24
Italian Front: Twelfth Battle of the Isonzo – Battle of Caporetto. In thick fog Austro-German troops make a surprise attack on Italian positions across a 20-mile front and breaking through at Tolmino, Caporetto, and Plezzo, pushing them back into Italy. taking 10,000 prisoners. During the Battle of Caporetto Italian troops disillusioned by the

conduct of the war and the harsh discipline of their officers desert and surrender en masse. Italy's fighting strength is halved and troops have to be sent from the Western Front to shore up the Italian lines.

25
Italian Front: Italians retreat across the Isonzo and start to evacuate the Bainsizza Plateau. Germans claim 30,000 prisoners.

26
Politics: Brazil declares war with Germany.

27
Western Front: United States infantry and artillery join in the action in France for the first time.

28
Italian Front: The Italian Second and Third

Arab Revolt
takes Aqaba
JUL

Third Battle of Ypres
(Passchendaele)
AUG

Germans take Riga
in the east
SEP

German Caporetto
offensive on
Italian Front
OCT

October Revolution
in Russia brings Lenin
to power;
Battle of Cambrai
NOV

Armistice on the
Eastern Front;
Allies take
Jerusalem
DEC

Canadian machine-gunners man shell holes in the mud on ground captured during the action at Broodseinde on 4 October 1917. They would imminently take part in the final attacks on Passchendaele ridge.

Bottom: American troops disembarking onto the quay at Liverpool. The first contingent arrived in autumn 1917.

Armies are in full retreat from the Carnia front. Germany claims to have taken 100,000 prisoners.

31

Middle East: Beersheba in Palestine, is occupied by British forces under the command of General Allenby, capturing 1,800 Turks. This starts a new offensive in Palestine.

November 1917

The October Revolution. The revolutionary Bolsheviks led by Lenin want to get out of the war. On the Italian Front the Italian Army is in retreat.

The third battle in front of Ypres between July and November 1917 was called Passchendaele.

1

Western Front: Germans abandon position on Chemin des Dames.

2

Politics: The Balfour Declaration. British Foreign Secretary Arthur Balfour sends a letter to Lord Rothschild affirming Britain's support for the creation of a Jewish state in Palestine after the war.

3

Western Front: Americans in trenches suffer 20 casualties in German attacks — the first U.S. soldiers todie from German attack.

6

Italian Front: Conference at Rapallo. Allied politicians and generals meet near Genoa to discuss what to do about the citical situation in Italy.

145

1917

Zimmerman telegram urges German ambassador to provoke war between Mexico and the U.S. **JAN**

U.S. breaks diplomatic relations with Germany **FEB**

Russian Revolution **MAR**

United States declares war on Germany **APR**

Pershing given command of AEF **MAY**

British offensive at Messines **J**

British soldiers keeping warm beside a roadside fire in the Cambrai area during winter 1917-18.

Mesopotamia: British forces led by General Maude reach and occupy Tekrit, 100 miles northwest of Bagdad.

Western Front: End of the Third Battle of Ypres as the village of Passchendaele is captured by Canadians after months of hard fighting.

7

Middle East: A force led by General Allenby captures Gaza in Palestine with support from British and French warships.

8

Russian Revolution: Bolshevik revolution in Russia — October Revolution (the Julian calendar was still in use in Russia). Vladimir Lenin and his supporters (including Trotsky) stage a nearly bloodless coup d'etat against the ineffective Kerensky Provisional Government. They seize Petrograd, depose Kerensky and form a Communist government with the intention of stopping Russian involvement in the war.

8

Italian Front: General Diaz succeeds General Cadorna as Commander-in-Chief of Italian armies.

9

Italian Front: The Rapallo Conference agrees on creating a Supreme Allied War Council to co-ordinate Allied actions on the Western Front.

10

Russian Revolution: Lenin becomes Premier of Russia, succeeding Kerensky.

Arab Revolt
takes Aqaba
JUL

Third Battle of Ypres
(Passchendaele)
AUG

Germans take Riga
in the east
SEP

German Caparetto
offensive on
Italian Front
OCT

October Revolution
in Russia brings Lenin
to power;
Battle of Cambrai
NOV

Armistice on the
Eastern Front;
Allies take
Jerusalem
DEC

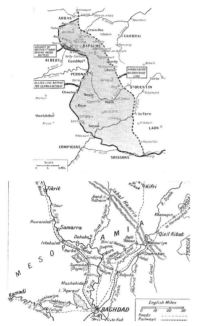

The front between Arras and Soissons. The shading shows how far the Germans retreated in 1917.

Bottom: The area around Baghdad, captured on November 18, 1817.

15

Politics: Georges Clemenceau becomes Premier of France (succeeding M. Painlove) and Minister of War.

Russian Revolution: Former premier Kerenski flees Moscow as bitter fighting breaks out.

16

Russian Revolution: A Bolshevik government is formed in Russia.

17

Middle East: In Palestine British troops capture Jaffa.

War at sea: Heligoland Bight Action. British battlecruiser attack on German minesweepers and covering heavy ships.

Joffre visiting the Italian General Cadorna on the Italian front.

18

Mesopotamia: General Sir Stanley Maude dies of cholera after drinking milky coffee.

20

Western Front: Battle of Cambrai starts with a surprise massed tank attack by the British when the Third Army under Lt. General Byng attack on a 10-mile front between the River Scarpe and St Quentin. During the attack, RFC aircraft drop bombs on anti-tank guns and strongpoints to clear a path for the Allied advance. The initial breakthrough cannot be supported and fails although over 8,000 prisoners are taken.

20

General: The Ukraine is declared a republic.

1917

Zimmerman telegram urges German ambassador to provoke war between Mexico and the U.S. **JAN**

U.S. breaks diplomatic relations with Germany **FEB**

Russian Revolution **MAR**

United States declares war on Germany **APR**

Pershing given command of AEF **MAY**

British offensive at Messines **JU**

Men of the Leicestershire Regiment (the Tigers) resting beside machine-gunners in a captured German trench near Ribécourt on the opening morning of the Cambrai offensive, 20 November 1917.

21

Western Front: Inter-Allied Conference in Paris creats a 'coalition diplomacy' of 18 nations. U.S. to be an 'associate' power with a separate army
Ribecourt, Flesquieres, Havrincourt, Marcoing and other German positions captured by British.

23

Italian Front: Italians repulse Germans on the whole front from the Asiago Plateau to the Brenta River.

24

Western Front: Cambrai menaced by the British, who approach within three miles, capturing Bourlon Wood.

25

Western Front: Many of the Battle of

Cambrai's initial gains by British are lost to German counter-attacks at Bourlon. Germans take 800 prisoners.

27

Africa: In East Africa near Nevala. Mahenge Force consisting of German and native troops under General Tafel surrender unconditionally.

30

Western Front: On the Cambrai front German attacks at Bourlon Wood, Moeuvres, and Vendhuille push the British back.

December 1917

Fighting ends on the Eastern Front as Russia and Germany sign a unilateral armistice. This allows Germany to move troops from the east to join the fighting on the Western Front.

Arab Revolt
takes Aqaba
JUL

Third Battle of Ypres
(Passchendaele)
AUG

Germans take Riga
in the east
SEP

German Caporetto
offensive on
Italian Front
OCT

October Revolution
in Russia brings Lenin
to power;
Battle of Cambrai
NOV

Armistice on the
Eastern Front;
Allies take
Jerusalem
DEC

Taken out of action by a shell, this burnt out British tank and its crew were casualties of the battle of Cambrai in November 1917.

Bottom: Clemenceau, French premier 1917–20, nicknamed the "Tiger", visits the front.

German soldiers marching into captivity following the third battle of Ypres.

Western Front: British retire from Bourlon Wood, Graincourt and other positions west of Cambrai.

1

Africa: German East Africa is reported to be completely conquered as von Lettow-Vorbeck pulls back across the Portuguese frontier of the Rovuma river.

Politics: First Inter-Allied Supreme War Council is held at Versailles with representatives from the United States, France, Great Britain and Italy,.

6

Politics: Finland declares its independence.

War at sea: In Halifax, Nova Scotia the Belgian ship Imo collides in harbor with the French ship Mont Blanc. Loaded with ammunition the latter caught fire and exploded taking most of Halifax with it – more than 1,900 people are killed,.

3

Russian Revolution: Russian Bolsheviks arrange a unilateral armistice with Germany.

7

Eastern Front: Germany, Austria-Hungary and Russia conclude an armistice on the Eastern Front, which will eventually release one million German soldiers for service on the Western Front.

5

Russian Revolution: Russia signs a preliminary suspension of hostilities with Germany.

149

1918

Strikes and riooting brings Austro-Hungarian Empire to its knees
JAN

Food rationing starts in England
FEB

German spring offensive –the Kaiserschlacht
MAR

Zeebrugge Raid
APR

U.S. forces in action for first time on Western Front at Cantigny
MAY

German offensive held at Battle of Chateau-Thie /Belleau W
JU

The official entry of General Allenby into Jerusalem was made on foot and through the Jaffa Gate on 11 December 1917.

Politics: The United States declares war against Austria-Hungary. Finland declares independence. Ecuador breaks off diplomatic relations with Germany.

9

Middle East: Jerusalem surrenders to British troops led by General Allenby. The Holy City had been held by the Turks for 673 years,.

10

Politics: Panama declares war against Austria-Hungary.

12

War at sea: Four German destroyers attack an Allied Scandinavian convoy southwest of Bjorne Fjord sinking the destroyer HMS Partridge and damaging HMS Pellew. Also sink all six merchantmen and two escorting trawlers.

15

Eastern Front: Armistice signed between the Central Powers and Russia at Brest-Litovsk.

17

Politics: Coalition government of Sir Robert Borden is returned andconsidered confirmed in Canada.

18

United States: Congress passes 18th Amendment for prohibition.

22

Politics: Russia opens separate peace negotiations with Germany (Brest-Litovsk).

23

War at sea: Four Harwich Force destroyers sail to meet a Dutch convoy off Maas Light Buoy. H MSs Torrent, Surprise, and Tornado

Second Battle
of the Marne
JUL

Allied offensive
on Western Front
begins
AUG

Hindenburg Line
positions breached;
Meuse-Argonne
offensive
SEP

Vittorio Veneto
offensive on
Italian Front;
Turkey surrenders
OCT

Armistice on
all fronts
NOV

President Wilson
arrives in Paris;
Yugoslavia created
DEC

Map of the Carso region Italy.

Bottom: Winter 1917-18: men of the Royal West Surrey Regiment in trenches near Arras.

hit mines, only Radiant survived. 193 men lost.

26
War at sea: In Britain Sir R. Wemyss is appointed First Sea Lord.

1918

January 1918
The Austro-Hunagrian Empire is starting to disintegrate as German forces are massing on the Western Front. Large numbers of German civilians stage protests against food shortages and the war. Some of the dispute's leaders are sent to the front but this only helps the dissent to spread. In the Middle East T.E. Lawrence (Lawrence of Arabia) leads Arab guerrillas in a successful campaign against

General Armando Diaz succeeded General Cadorna in command of the Italian armies after the disaster of Caporetto.

Turkish positions in Arabia and Palestine.

8
United States: President Wilson addresses a joint session of Congress and delivers his 'Fourteen Points' requirements for peace. These include the need for open diplomacy, freedom of the seas, reduction of armaments and the removal of economic barriers. He also specifies the restoration of Belgium and the independence of Poland.

10
United States: U.S. House passed the Nineteenth Amendment allowing women the vote – ratified in 1920.

12
War at sea: Destroyers Narbrough, Opal wrecked entering Scapa Flow – pitch black

1918

Strikes and riooting brings Austro-Hungarian Empire to its knees
JAN

Food rationing starts in England
FEB

German spring offensive —the Kaiserschlacht
MAR

Zeebrugge Raid
APR

U.S. forces in action for first time on Western Front at Cantigny
MAY

German offensive held at Battle of Chateau-Thie [Belleau W
JU

Troops of the Manchester Regiment take refuge behind a stranded British tank.

night, blizzard, ploughed into rocks, one survivor.

14
Politics: Ex Premier Joseph Caillaux is arrested for treason in Paris.

15
Western Front: st Division of AEF at Ansauville.

16
Politics: In Vienna and Budapest strikes and riots break out showing citizens' frustrations and dissatisfaction with the war.

20
War at sea: The Mittelmeerdivision is wrecked in the Dardanelles. The cruiser Breslau is sunk by a mine, and Goeben damaged in a minefield (a few days later) after attacking

British naval forces at Imbros. British monitor Raglan and monitor M28 are also sunk.

24
Palestine: Arab (Hejaz) forces are victorious over the Turks near Tafila.

28
Politics: Civil war breaks out in Finland started by a Bolshevik coup in Helsinki.

29
United States: Prohibition ratified in the United States to come into effect on 20 January, 1920.

February 1918
Turkey reoccupies the Caucasus.

Second Battle
of the Marne
JUL

Allied offensive
on Western Front
begins
AUG

Hindenburg Line
positions breached;
Meuse–Argonne
offensive
SEP

Vittorio Veneto
offensive on
Italian Front;
Turkey surrenders
OCT

Armistice on
all fronts
NOV

President Wilson
arrives in Paris;
Yugoslavia created
DEC

"I am the Hun's Father Christmas".
Bottom: Palestine 1918.

Allenby would become a viscount for his victory in Palestine in 1917–18.

1

General: Russia adopts the Gregorian Calendar.

War at sea: The Austro-Hungarian navy mutinies at the southern Adriatic port of Cattaro.

5

War at sea: U.S. troop carrier Tuscania is torpedoed off the Irish coast with the loss of 166.

6

Politics: In Romania the Bratianu cabinet resigns.

8

Politics: General Alexandru Averescu becomes the new prime minister of Romania.

9

Politics: On the former Eastern Front a peace treaty is signed between the Central Powers and Ukraine Rada: the 'Brotfrieden' Peace, and the Ukranian frontiers are defined.

10

Politics: Trotsky announces that Russia will take no further part in the war and will immediately demobilize.

11

Politics: U.S. President Woodrow Wilson makes his 'Four Principles' speech, restating his war aims to a joint session of Congress.

16

General: General Sir Henry Wilson (PM Lloyd George's supporter) replaces General Sir William Robertson (Haig's main supporter) as British chief of staff.

1918

Strikes and riooting
brings Austro-Hungarian
Empire to its knees
JAN

Food rationing
starts in England
FEB

German spring
offensive
—the Kaiserschlacht
MAR

Zeebrugge Raid
APR

U.S. forces in action
for first time on
Western Front
at Cantigny
MAY

German offensive
held at Battle of
Chateau-Thi
/Belleau
J

Canadian troops on exercise.

Politics: Lithuania declares its independence from both Russia and Germany.

17

Eastern Front: Operation 'Faustschlag' — a limited German offensive to destabilze the Bolshevik government.

Western Front: In an air raid on London 21 people are killed and a further 32 injured.

21

Middle East: In Palestine British forces take Jericho.

24

Caucasus: Turks reoccupy Trebizond.

26

War at sea: In the Bristol Channel the hospital ship Glenart Castle is torpedoed. 162 lives are lost.

Western Front:
Eight U.S. soldiers die from a gas attack.

March 1918

Germany starts the great Spring Offensive. The Allies had warning from RFC reconnaissance flights which reported that enemy units were being relieved by fresh units — a sure sign that an attack was imminent. Germany won air superiority over the Somme with their c.730 aircraft, of which 326 are fighter planes, while the RFC faced it with 579 aircraft, of which 261 are fighters. Against the French, the Germans had an additional 367 aircraft while the French had around 2,000.

Top: Under cover of a smoke screen, German storm troopers prepare to attack. On the right a dog with a message tied to its collar takes a progress report back to HQ.

Bottom: German troops preparing to go over the top. They carried entrenching tools and would move with rifles slung so they could easily throw grenades.

1
Eastern Front: German forces occupy Kiev.

3
Eastern Front/Western Front: Treaty of Brest-Litovsk signed between Bolshevik Russia and the Central Powers in separate peace negotiations. Russia hands over 25 percent of its territory. All prisoners of war are to be sent home. This frees troops from the Eastern Front and they are sent instead to the Western Front where, for a short while, the Central Powers enjoy numerical superiority.

5
Balkans: Romania signs a preliminary peace treaty with the Central Powers at Buftea, ceding land, making concessions and agreeing to demobilize.

Russian Revolution: The Soviet Union moves the national capital from Petrograd to Moscow.

6
General: Finnish Airforce founded.

11
Caucasus: In Armenia Turkish forces reoccupy Erzurum.

12
Far East: Fighting between Japanese and Chinese troops on the Russian Manchurian border.

13
Caucasus: The Central Powers occupy the Black Sea port of Odessa in south Ukraine.

1918

Strikes and rioting brings Austro-Hungarian Empire to its knees **JAN**

Food rationing starts in England **FEB**

German spring offensive —the Kaiserschlacht **MAR**

Zeebrugge Raid **APR**

U.S. forces in action for first time on Western Front at Cantigny **MAY**

German offensive held at Battle of Chateau-Thierry /Belleau ... J

A wounded British soldier is carried back over a support line in the Somme. French troops man machine guns in the trenches beneath.

21

Western Front: Start of German Spring Offensive aka the 'Kaiserschlacht.' Von Ludendorff launches a major series of offensives along a 50-mile front south of Arras between the rivers Sensée and Oise in an effort to gain a decisive victory before the arrival of American troops on the Western Front. Major successes are reported. The first attack made against the British – the Michael offensive – develops into the Battle of Picardy. Eventually there are five major offensives against Allied forces. This massive offensive became possible when Germany shifted 40 divisions from the Eastern Front to West. Thousands of British troops were captured on the first day as others were pushed back to the Crozat Canal. By nightfall 17 RFC squadrons were forced to evacuate airfields in danger of being overrun by oncoming enemy forces.

22

War at sea: Sloop Gaillardia mined in Northern Barrage.
Allies inform the Dutch government that they intend to seize all Dutch ships in Allied ports.

Western Front: British lines west of St Quentin are broken and Allies lose 40 miles. Germans claim 16,000 prisoners. German forces reach the Somme.

23

Middle East: In Transjordan British forces attack.

Western Front: German offensive redirects towards Amiens and Paris. They capture Péronne and Ham and reach the line of the Somme. German forces attempt to capture Amiens, an important link in the French rail network. Paris comes under long range attack

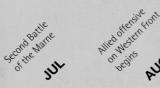

Second Battle of the Marne
JUL

Allied offensive on Western Front begins
AUG

Hindenburg Line positions breached; Meuse-Argonne offensive
SEP

Vittorio Veneto offensive on Italian Front; Turkey surrenders
OCT

Armistice on all fronts
NOV

President Wilson arrives in Paris; Yugoslavia created
DEC

German troops advance in Spring 1918.

Bottom: Allied battery of 18-pounder guns moving towards Mailly-Maillet three days after the German offensive in March 1918.

from Big Bertha, a 43-ton mobile howitzer, firing from 74 miles away.

Air activity intensifies with up to 70 aircraft involved in a single air combat. RFC and RNAS squadrons carry out low level attacks against German targets causing great disruption. By the end of the month this continued pressure causes the German advance to falter – the first time large scale use of air power had had a direct influence on the outcome of a battle.

25

Western Front: After fierce fighting around Bapaume the Germans take the town in a night attack. Claim to have collected 45,000 Allied prisoners since the start of the Spring Offensive.

Men of the London Scottish, part of the 56th Division, move back from the line, March 30, 1918.

26

Western Front: Allies hold a crisis conference at Doullens to discuss unity of command. The Doullens Agreement gives Marshal Ferdinand Foch 'co-ordinating authority' over all Allied troops on the Western Front.

Heavy fighting both north and south of the Somme. British lose Albert and Bray.

Noyon, Lihons, Chaulnes, and Roye are lost to German attacks.

The British use Whippet tanks in action for the first time.

A quarter of a million American troops are now based in France and a further 250,000 will arrive every month until the end of the war.

28

Western Front: An intense German attack along a wide front on the River Scarpe fails with heavy losses and the German advance is

157

1918

Strikes and rioting brings Austro-Hungarian Empire to its knees
JAN

Food rationing starts in England
FEB

German spring offensive —the Kaiserschlacht
MAR

Zeebrugge Raid
APR

U.S. forces in action for first time on Western Front at Cantigny
MAY

German offensive held at Battle c Chateau-Th /Belleau \
J

Marshal Foch was appointed chief of the Allied forces in March 1918.

checked. This, the first AEF success, proves to be the turning point of the war.

April 1918

The success of the German Spring Offensive brings new unity and resolve among both civilians and the military.

1

General: In Britain, the Royal Air Force and Women's Royal Air Force are formed from the Royal Flying Corps and Royal Naval Air Service.

4

Western Front: The Germans make the final Kaiserschlacht attack towards Amiens.

5

Western Front: The German offensive is halted outside Amiens by a combined British and Australian force. Ludendorff calls off the Michael Offensive.

8

Politics: In Rome the Conference of Nationalities Oppressed by Austria opens.

9

Western Front: The Second Spring offensive, codenamed 'Georgette', starts with the Battle of the Lys as Germany launches its attack with a heavy bombardment at Ypres in the British sector of Armentières. The very heavy fighting along a line from La Bassée Canal to Armentières forces British and Portuguese troops back.

9

Politics: French premier Clémenceau publishes Kaiser Karl's 1917 attempts to make peace.

Second Battle of the Marne
JUL

Allied offensive on Western Front begins
AUG

Hindenburg Line positions breached; Meuse–Argonne offensive
SEP

Vittorio Veneto offensive on Italian Front; Turkey surrenders
OCT

Armistice on all fronts
NOV

President Wilson arrives in Paris; Yugoslavia created
DEC

British Whippet tanks came into service in March 1918. The one shown was used by Brig-Gen V.W. Odium of 11th Canadian Infantry Brigade, part of 4th Division, on reconnaissance duties. It is on the Arras–Cambrai road; alongside are Canadian infantry.

Bottom: 43rd Casualty Clearing Station at Frévent 20 miles east of Arras, seen on April 8, 1918.

Long train of cattle trucks containing Allied infantry reinforcements at St Eloi on 1 April 1918.

14

Politics: General Foch is appointed Commander-in-Chief of all Allied forces on the Western Front in France.

15

Caucasus: In Transcaucasia Turkish forces take Batum.

Politics: Austro-Hungarian Foreign Minister Count Czernin resigns and is replaced by Count Istvan Burian von Rajecz.

Western Front: Bailleul and Wulverghem captured by the Germans. Very heavy artillery action on the Somme.

16

Western Front: Wytschaete and Meteren lost to the Germans and retaken within the day.

17

Middle East: In Arabia the Arab Army besiege Maan.

Western Front: Wytschaete and Meteren lost again.

21

Western Front: Baron Manfred von Richtofen, aka 'The Red Baron', is shot down and killed near Corbie. The top scoring fighter pilot of World War I with 80 kills, his kill was variously claimed by Australian gunners and by a Canadian pilot.

1918

Strikes and rioting
brings Austro-Hungarian
Empire to its knees
JAN

Food rationing
starts in England
FEB

German spring
offensive
—the Kaiserschlacht
MAR

Zeebrugge Raid
APR

U.S. forces in action
for first time on
Western Front
at Cantigny
MAY

German offensive
held at Battle of
Chateau-Thi
/Belleau

Hall 3 at the zeppelin base of Ahlhorn after British bombing.

22–23

Western Front: During a night raid the Allies attack Zeebrugge and Ostend harbors being used as German naval bases. Zeebrugge harbor entrance was blocked by obselete cruisers Thetis, Intrepid, Iphigenia which were filled with concrete and blown up, along with submarine C.3 which was exploded on the Mole. The destroyer North Star was hit by a shore battery and scuttled. At Ostend the cruiser blockships Brilliant, and Sirius, were run ashore and blown up and fail to block the entrance as planned.

23

Politics: Guatemala declares war on Germany.

War at sea: Last sortie for the German High Seas Fleet.

Western Front: Heavy German attacks gain Villers-Bretonneux.

24

War at sea: German Battlecruiser Moltke of the High Seas Fleet loses a screw while out on a sortie to attack Scandinavian convoy routes. As the Fleet returns, Moltke is torpedoed by E.42.

28

Eastern Front: In Finland the Red Army is defeated at the Battle of Viborg.

29

Western Front: End of the Battle of the Lys: in spite of heavy German artillery three British divisions hold off 13 German infantry divisions who sustain heavy losses.

Second Battle of the Marne

JUL

Allied offensive on Western Front begins

AUG

Hindenburg Line positions breached; Meuse-Argonne offensive

SEP

Vittorio Veneto offensive on Italian Front; Turkey surrenders

OCT

Armistice on all fronts

NOV

President Wilson arrives in Paris; Yugoslavia created

DEC

Baron Manfred von Richthofen, the 'Red Baron'. He destroyed 80 Allied planes before being shot down on 21 April 1918, behind Australian lines near the Somme.
Below: Australian troops present arms as von Richthofen's coffin passes by carried on the shoulders of RAF officers.

30
Middle East: Start of the second British attack in Transjordan.

May 1918
American troops join the fighting on the Western Front for the first time as Paris comes under direct threat of German attacks and occupation.

1
Western Front: American troops join the front line on the Amiens front.

7
Politics: The Peace of Bucharest is signed between Romania and the Central Powers.

British troops man "Archies" (anti-aircraft guns), near Armentiéres.

Romania cedes territory and immediately demobilizes the army.
Nicaragua declares war on Germany.

10
Western Front: British attack on Ostend when the cruiser HMS Vindictive was filled with concrete and sunk in the harbor entrance. German cruisers were from then on unable to use the harbor and other shipping greatly inconvenienced.

11
Politics: Kaiser Karl I of Austria accepts economic and military union with Germany.

19–20
Western Front: Germany mounts its largest (and ultimately last) aircraft raid on Britain, killing 49 and injuring 177 people. From a total of 43 bombers dispatched, 33 actually

161

1918

Strikes and riooting brings Austro-Hungarian Empire to its knees
JAN

Food rationing starts in England
FEB

German spring offensive –the Kaiserschlacht
MAR

Zeebrugge Raid
APR

U.S. forces in action for first time on Western Front at Cantigny
MAY

German offensive held at Battle Chateau-Thi /Belleau

A line of disabled soldiers at a dressing station at Béthune. They have been temporarily blinded by lachrymatory gas deployed by the Germans during the Lys offensive.

carry out the raid. Six were lost – two to intercepting fighters, three to anti-aircraft fire and one due to engine failure over Essex.

25
Politics: Costa Rica declares war on Germany.

War at sea: German U-boats appear in U.S. waters for first time.

26
Caucasus: Armenia signs the Treaty of Batum with Turkey.

27
Western Front: Third German Spring offensive – codenamed 'Blucher' – launched in the French sector along Chemin des Dames on the Aisne. Starts the Third Battle of the Aisne. The French are pushed back to the Marne as the Germans try to get to Paris.

28
Western Front: U.S. forces – 28th Regiment of the 1st Division – are victorious in their first major independent operation at the Battle of Cantigny.

29
Western Front: German troops advance to the Marne but are stopped by U.S. Divisions. French driven back across Aisne, and Germans capture Soissons.

30
Western Front: Germans reach the Marne.

31
War at sea: Destroyer Fairy lost ramming and sinking UC75 off Flamborough Head.

June 1918
From June to October Anglo-American forces

Second Battle of the Marne
JUL

Allied offensive on Western Front begins
AUG

Hindenburg Line positions breached; Meuse-Argonne offensive
SEP

Vittorio Veneto offensive on Italian Front; Turkey surrenders
OCT

Armistice on all fronts
NOV

President Wilson arrives in Paris; Yugoslavia created
DEC

Dressing station in the Bois l'Abbé during the German attack on Amiens, May 27, 1918.

Below: US troops of 1st Division's 28th Infantry in an ambush position at Bonvillers on May 22, 1918.

started laying the 69,000 mines known as the Northern Barrage which was designed to stop U-boat traffic between the Orkneys and Norway.
On the Western Front the German advances are halted while on the Southern Front the Italian forces manage to hold off the Austro-Hungarian attacks.

2
Western Front: End of the Second Battle of the Aisne. Heavy fighting at Ourcq and the front moves backward and forward as attacks are successful or repulsed. American forces stop German attempt to cross the Marne River at Château-Thierry.

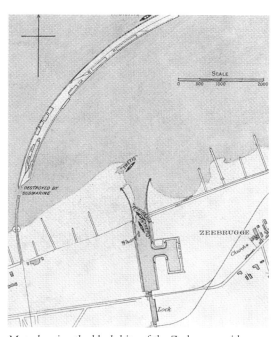

Map showing the blockships of the Zeebrugge raid.

4
Politics: Baron de Broqueville resigns as the premier of Belgium after losing the support of his own party.

Western Front: Chateâu-Thierry retaken – the first battle that AEF forces play a decisive role. U.S. forces also check German advance at Veuilly Wood.

6
Western Front: US 3rd Division captures Bouresches and southern part of Belleau Wood. American forces suffer heavy losses but defeat Germans.

8
Great Britain: The British Independent Air Force was formed for strategic bombing.

1918

Strikes and riooting brings Austro-Hungarian Empire to its knees
JAN

Food rationing starts in England
FEB

German spring offensive –the Kaiserschlacht
MAR

Zeebrugge Raid
APR

U.S. forces in action for first time on Western Front at Cantigny
MAY

German offensive held at Battle of Chateau-Thie /Belleau W
JU

Map of Britain showing hostile air raid and naval bombardments between 16 December 1914 and 17 June 1918.

War at sea: U.S. steamer Pinar del Rio sunk by German U-boat off Maryland.
The first mines are laid in the Northern Barrage. The new proximity triggered American magnetic mines only claimed three known submarines as German sub commanders easily found ways through the barrier.

9

War at sea: In the Adriatic the Austro-Hungarian dreadnought Szent Istvan is torpedoed.

Western Front: Start of the First Battle of Lassigny as Germans launch a new offensive toward Compiègne on a line between Noyon and Montdidier. German Eighteenth Army launch the Fourth Spring Offensive, Battle of the Matz – aka Battle of Noyon – in the French sector between Noyan and Montdider.

German forces attack towards Compiègne – the Gneisenau offensive.

11

Western Front: German advance checked.

13

Western Front: End of the First Battle of Lassigny.

14

Western Front: The German offensive on the Western Front ends.

15

Italian Front: Start of the Second Battle of the Piave River starts with a massive Austrian attack stretching from Lagarina Valley to the sea. They are eventually defeated by a combined Anglo-French and Italian force and sustain very heavy losses.

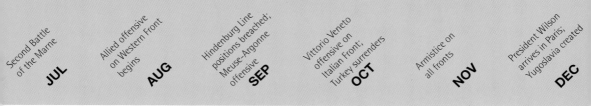

May 28, 1918: British troops retreat through Passy-sur-Marne.

Bottom: American troops rush to the front in May 1918. They are passing through Montmirail.

16

Politics: Alexander Malinov replaces Vasil Radoslavov as prime minister of Bulgaria.

18

Italian Front: The flooded Piave river foils Austrain attempts to get across.

23

Italian Front: End of the Second Battle of the Piave as the Austrians retreat in disorder from Montello to the sea.

27

War at sea: Southwest of Fastnet the hospital ship Llandovery Castle is torpedoed. 244 lives are lost.

German troops advance in Spring 1918.

July 1918.

The Allies start to get the upper hand on the Western Front and begin to intervene on the Eastern Front in Russia. In the west German submarine undersea warfare completely fails to stop U.S. soldiers being moved across the Atlantic to join the war effort against the Central Powers. The first cases of influenza start to appear in the German trenches.

2

Politics: Allied Supreme War Council supports intervention in Siberia.

United States: President Wilson announces that a million American soldiers have been sent to Europe.

4

Politics: Ottoman Emperor Mehmed V (Resad), Sultan of Turkey dies and is succeeded by

165

1918

Strikes and riooting brings Austro-Hungarian Empire to its knees
JAN

Food rationing starts in England
FEB

German spring offensive −the Kaiserschlacht
MAR

Zeebrugge Raid
APR

U.S. forces in action for first time on Western Front at Cantigny
MAY

German offensive held at Battle of Chateau-Thie /Belleau W
JI

Carrier tank passes a Scottish working party.

Mehmed VI (Vahid-ed-Din) as Sultan.

Western Front: Battle of Le Hamel. Successful small Australian offensive east of Amiens.

6
United States: U.S. President Woodrow Wilson agrees to American intervention in Siberia.

8
Politics: German Foreign Minister Richard von Kühlmann is dismissed for his 'defeatist' political views.

12
War at sea: While at anchor in Tokuyama Bay the Japanese dreadnought Kawachi explodes: 500 lost.

15
Western Front: Final phase of Great German Spring push starts the Second Battle of Marne. Von Ludendorf's final offensive − the Friedensturm − is on a front 50-miles long east and west of Reims. In reply the Allies start amassing a major strike force in northern France to hit back.

16
Russian Revolution: Former Tsar Nicholas II, his wife, and children, are shot and murdered by the Bolsheviks at Ekaterinenburg the capital of the Red Ural, by order of the Ural Regional Council.

18
Western Front: Massive Allied counterattack including nine U.S. divisions hit back against German forces south-west of the Marne. The Allies attacked along a 27-mile front between

Second Battle of the Marne
JUL

Allied offensive on Western Front begins
AUG

Hindenburg Line positions breached; Meuse-Argonne offensive
SEP

Vittorio Veneto offensive on Italian Front; Turkey surrenders
OCT

Armistice on all fronts
NOV

President Wilson arrives in Paris; Yugoslavia created
DEC

June 15, 1918: the German High Command clebrate the 30th anniversary of the Kaiser's accession. Left front is Ludendorff; central are Hundenurg and Prince Henry of Prussia; behind him the Kaiser.

Bottom: Stokes mortar set up in a captured trench, July 9, 1918.

Fontenoy and Belleau and seized the strategic initiative.

19

Politics: Honduras declares war against Germany.

Western Front: German forces start to retreat at the Marne — having failed to make the key breakthrough — back to the Hindenburg Line.

24

Politics: Baron Hussarek becomes premier of Austria, succeeding Count von Clam-Martinic.

The Tsar and 11-year old Tsarevich both in Cossack uniform.

30

Eastern Front: In Kiev the German military dictator Field Marshall Hermann von Eichorn commander of occupying forces in the Ukraine and the Crimea, is assassinated by nationalist rebels.

31

Arctic: Anglo-French soldiers take the strategically import port of Archangel on the White Sea and capture the defenses.

August 1918

'Spanish Flu' influenza, becomes pandemic; over twenty-five million people will die in the following six months (three times as many as died during the war). Despite influenza among the troops Allied counter-offenses are begun on the Western Front.

The RAF start flying offensive fighter sweeps across the Western Front using either Sopwith

1918

Strikes and rioting
brings Austro-Hungarian
Empire to its knees
JAN

Food rationing
starts in England
FEB

German spring
offensive
—the Kaiserschlacht
MAR

Zeebrugge Raid
APR

U.S. forces in action
for first time on
Western Front
at Cantigny
MAY

German offensive
held at Battle of
Chateau-Thie
/Belleau W
JL

German field guns captured in the Franco-American advance around Soissons in July 1918 turned against their former owners.

Camels flying at 10,000 feet, SE5s at 14,000 feet, or Bristol Fighters at 18,000 feet.

2

War at sea: Admiral Franz von Hipper becomes as c-in-c of the High Seas Fleet replacing Admiral Reinhardt Scheer who moves on to become German Naval Supreme Commander.

3

Far East: Large-scale British intervention begins at Vladivostok — the Russian far eastern port on the Sea of Japan — to support the Czech Legion against Bolshevik forces.

4

Western Front: Second Battle of the Marne ends as U.S. troops take Fismes and the Allies secure the right bank of the Vesle.

6

Great Britain: Four German airships carry out the last air raid on Britain over East Anglia. One, carrying the head of the German Naval Airship Service, was shot down near Kings Lynn, Norfolk. No British casualties or damage reported.

8

Western Front: Second Battle of Amiens starts with a massive Anglo-French attack with 2,070 guns and 342 Mark V heavy tanks and 72 Whippet medium tanks across a 15-mile front from Morlancourt to Montdidier. Directed by General Haig the British Fourth and French First armies achieve major successes forcing the Germans back to the Hindenburg Line. The Germans sustain 27,000 casualties on the first day alone and are pushed back eight miles. General Erich Ludendorff later describes it as 'the Black Day'

Second Battle of the Marne
JUL

Allied offensive on Western Front begins
AUG

Hindenburg Line positions breached; Meuse-Argonne offensive
SEP

Vittorio Veneto offensive on Italian Front; Turkey surrenders
OCT

Armistice on all fronts
NOV

President Wilson arrives in Paris; Yugoslavia created
DEC

Men from Allenby's Palestinian command were transferred to France via Egypt and Italy to help stem the German March 1918 offensive. This crowded troopship is somewhere in the Mediterranean.

Bottom: French tank in July 1918 at Battle of Maque.

of the German army. Heavy fighting results in losses of around a quarter of all aircraft.

American troops continue to come into Europe in 1918. Here a troopship disembarks at Liverpool docks.

12

Western Front: Close of the Battle of Amiens resulting in heavy defeat for the Germans. The German General Staff realize that the end is in sight.

U.S. forces make first attack under independent command.

9

Western Front: Second Battle of Lassigny starts as the French Third Army advance on Montdidier and the British occupy Morlancourt.

13

Politics: Great Britain recognizes the independence of Czechoslovakia.

11

War at sea: British raid on Heligoland Bight shipping by six motor torpedo boats covered by Harwich Force and planned air cover. Three motor torpedo boats sunk by German aircraft, two damaged.
The Japanese Navy arrives at Vladivostok.

14

Western Front: Germans start to retreat from positions around the River Ancre. They evacuate Beaumont-Hamel, Bucqoy, Serre, and Puisieux.

16

Far East: Japanese General Otani lands at Vladivostok at the head of Japanese troops.

Strikes and riooting
brings Austro-Hungarian
Empire to its knees

JAN

Food rationing
starts in England

FEB

German spring
offensive
—the Kaiserschlacht

MAR

Zeebrugge Raid

APR

U.S. forces in action
for first time on
Western Front
at Cantigny

MAY

German offensive
held at Battle of
Chateau-Thie
(Belleau W

JU

The tide had turned: German prisoners at Abbeville, August 27, 1914.

17

Far East: U.S. soldiers land at Vladivostok to join the Allied contingent.

Western Front: French troops begin successful drive to push the Germans off the Aisne Heights.

21

Western Front: second Battle of Albert: Battle of Bapaume begins as the British Third and Fourth armies attack north of the Ancre on a 10-mile front from Beaucourt-sur-Ancre and Moyenneville.

22

Western Front: British recapture Albert and the Bray-Albert road.

25

Caucasus: In Baku, 'Dunsterforce' comprising almost 1,000 elite British, Canadian, Australian, and New Zealand troops assemble.

26

Western Front: Scarpe Offensive. This supporting operation starts with the British First Army attack on German positions on the River Scarpe that successfully captured the strongpoint of Monchy-le-Preux.

29

Russian Revolution: Lenin the Bolshevik leader escapes an assassination attempt depite being wounded. The damage affects his health for the rest of his life.

Western Front: French recapture Noyon and British recapture Bapaume.

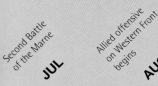

Second Battle of the Marne
JUL

Allied offensive on Western Front begins
AUG

Hindenburg Line positions breached; Meuse-Argonne offensive
SEP

Vittorio Veneto offensive on Italian Front; Turkey surrenders
OCT

Armistice on all fronts
NOV

President Wilson arrives in Paris; Yugoslavia created
DEC

Four pictures showing a patrol by men of the 6th Seaforth Highlanders. First, drawing bombs; second, heading out from the trench line; third/fourth, looking into German dugouts; Battle of the Scarpe, August 29, 1918.

Bottom: Dunsterforce at Baku in August 1918.

British armoured cars on August 25, 1918.

continue their successful advance north of Noyon.

31

Western Front: End of the Battle of Bapaume as the Germans evacuate Mt. Kemmel.

September 1918

Allied air power continues in support of offensives against the Hindenberg Line, Germany's last line of defense, Between 11 and 15 September, 1,483 aircraft of all kinds are used in the assault on St. Mihiel Salient during the Battle of Bapaume.

1

Western Front: British capture Péronne. Announce that during August they captured over 57,000 German prisoners and 650 guns. French retake Coucy, Juvigny, Leury as they

2

Western Front: Despite fierce fighting along a 23-mile front the British First Army supported by tanks break through the Drocourt-Quéant 'switch' line and capture Cagnicourt, Villers, and Quéant.

3

Politics: The U.S.A. recognizes Czechoslovakia.

Western Front: End of the Battle of the Scarpe as the Germans evacuate back toward the Hindenburg Line in the face of the British advance. Elsewhere the French cross the Somme at Épenancourt.

1918

Strikes and riooting
brings Austro-Hungarian
Empire to its knees
JAN

Food rationing
starts in England
FEB

German spring
offensive
—the Kaiserschlacht
MAR

Zeebrugge Raid
APR

U.S. forces in action
for first time on
Western Front
at Cantigny
MAY

German offensive
held at Battle of
Chateau-Thi
/Belleau W
J

British Mark V tanks advance near Bellicourt, September 29, 1918.

4

Far East: After fierce fighting against German troops the Allied force occupies Oboserskaia, 73 miles south of Archangel.

Western Front: A British force takes the Canal du Nord. The British also retake Ploegsteert, Bailleul, Kemmel, and Neuve Chapelle.

12

Western Front: Start of the Battle of Epéhy on the Cambrai front.
Battle of St. Mihiel takes place through strong winds and heavy rain. American forces supported by French troops attack, clear, and occupy the St. Mihiel salient, in the process taking over 13,000 prisoners. During the battle despite the appaling weather conditions. the U.S. launches the greatest air assault of the war The AEF took 15,000 prisoners at St. Mihiel in Sept.

Battle of Havrincourt. Three British divisions capture the village from four German divisions.

14

Caucasus: The British evacuate from Baku.

Western Front: Kaiser Karl of Austria-Hungary informs the German Kaiser that he wants to enter into peace negotiations with the Allies. By this stage the Austro-Hungarian Empire is starting to disintegrate.

15

Balkans: A Franco-Serbian offensive against Bulgarian positions begins the Battle of the Vardar. The Allies prevail and take 800 prisoners.

Second Battle of the Marne
JUL

Allied offensive on Western Front begins
AUG

Hindenburg Line positions breached; Meuse-Argonne offensive
SEP

Vittorio Veneto offensive on Italian Front; Turkey surrenders
OCT

Armistice on all fronts
NOV

President Wilson arrives in Paris; Yugoslavia created
DEC

General Pershing became the hero of St Mihiel in September 1918 when the U.S. Army first proved its worth.

Bottom: An American regiment marches through the St Mihiel salient on September 12 and 13, 1918.

German prisoners head towards a POW cage, August 8, 1918.

17

Middle East: Dera, an important railroad junction in Palestine, is surrounded by 5,000 Northern Arab Army forces.

18

Western Front: Start of the Battle of Epéhy as the British Fourth Army attacks forward outposts of the Hindenburg Line.

19

Middle East: In Palestine the British start a great offensive to drive Turkey out of Syria and Palestine. Battle of Megiddo aka the Battle of Armageddon. Allied troops under General Allenby advance across a 16-mile front from Rafat to the sea.

21

Middle East: RAF aircraft in Palestine attack and destroy the retreating Turkish Seventh Army at Wadi el Fara.

22

Balkans: Serbians attack Bulgarian troops and force them to retreat all along a 100-mile front from Monastir to Lake Dorian.

23

Middle East: British 15th Cavalry Brigade attacks Haifa.

25

Balkans: End of the Battle of the Vardar. Battered and routed by the Serbs and their Allies, Bulgaria proposes an armistice but the c-in-c General Franchet d'Esperey refuses to stop his advance.

1918

Strikes and riooting brings Austro-Hungarian Empire to its knees
JAN

Food rationing starts in England
FEB

German spring offensive –the Kaiserschlacht
MAR

Zeebrugge Raid
APR

U.S. forces in action for first time on Western Front at Cantigny
MAY

German offensive held at Battle Chateau-T/Belleau

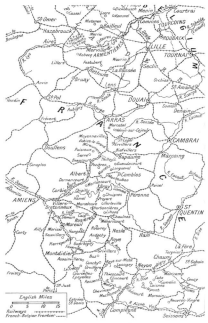

Map of the ground over which British and French troops advanced after August 8, 1918.

US troops from the 7th Infantry Regiment.

Politics: Italy recognizes Yugoslavian independence.

26

Balkans: In Bulgaria British troops enter Strumitsa. Fierce fighting between Serbs and Bulgarians for Usküb.

Western Front: Massive (and final) Franco-American offensive along a 40-mile front from Champagne to the Meuse. This is the greatest offensive of the war for U.S. troops as they attack in the Argonne in eatsren France. The massive Allied attack breaks through the Hindenburg Line. Although victorious the U.S. troops take heavy casualties as General Pershing loses 120,000 (about 10 percent) of his men.

27

Western Front: British attack on German lines at Cambrai sets off the Second Battle of Cambrai and specifically the Battle of St. Quentin. Again the Hindenburg Line is broken and the British make gains: Canadians capture Bourlon Wood.
Continued successes for French and U.S. forces as they advance between Reims and Verdun and converge on the Argonne.
Canal du Nord Offensive by the British First Army on the Siegfried Stellung, the strongest part part of the Hindenburg Line.

28

Africa: Lettow-Vorbeck re-enters German East Africa with his Schutztruppe.

Balkans: Bulgaria signs an armistice with the Allies. When Ludendorff learns of the capitulation he suffers a seizure.

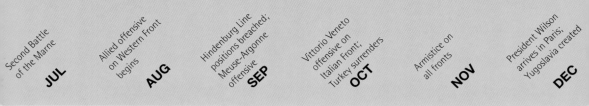

Second Battle
of the Marne
JUL

Allied offensive
on Western Front
begins
AUG

Hindenburg Line
positions breached;
Meuse-Argonne
offensive
SEP

Vittorio Veneto
offensive on
Italian Front;
Turkey surrenders
OCT

Armistice on
all fronts
NOV

President Wilson
arrives in Paris;
Yugoslavia created
DEC

Female munition worker regulating a lathe. Behind her are piled shell cases in various stages of completion.

Italian Front: East of Condé Italians force the crossing of the Aisne.

Western Front: The Battle of Flanders begins with a successful Anglo-Belgian attack (led by King Albert) along a 23-mile front from Dixmude to Ploegsteert. They capture Houthulst Forest and more than 4,000 German prisoners.
U.S. forces retake many villages as they advance despite fierce fighting in the Argonne to Exermont and Brieulles.

29

Western Front: The Allies break through the Hindenburg Line – Germany's last fixed line of defense on the Western Front – and cross the St. Quentin canal.

Map showing the Caucasus area, the scene of final British operations in 1918.

30

Africa: Bulgaria surrenders to the Allies and accepts their peace terms.

Middle East: British and Arab troops take Damascus and so end the Battle of Samaria. They capture 7,000 prisoners.

October 1918

Allies continue their successful offensives as many German forces are forced backward. Italian troops finally drive Austro-Hungarian soldiers out of Italy. Turkey surrenders to the Allies.

1

Middle East: In Palestine British and Arab forces occupy Damascus.

1918

Strikes and rioting brings Austro-Hungarian Empire to its knees
JAN

Food rationing starts in England
FEB

German spring offensive —the Kaiserschlacht
MAR

Zeebrugge Raid
APR

U.S. forces in action for first time on Western Front at Cantigny
MAY

German offensive held at Battle of Chateau-Thi /Belleau J

British troops recapture Cambrai, October 9, 1918.

Western Front: Ludendorff summons his senior officers to his headquarters at Spa and tells them that Germany must request an immediate ceasefire.
French retake part of St. Quentin and advance remorselessly through Champagne.The Germans retreat back from the Reims-Aisne plateau.

2

Western Front: French troops capture St Quentin.

4

Politics: Prince Max von Baden is appointed Chancellor of Germany.
Joint Austro-German peace note to U.S. President Woodrow Wilson requests an armistice based on his '14 Points.'.
King Ferdinand of Bulgaria abdicates in favor of his son Boris. The latter then signs the

order for the demobilization of the Bulgarian Army.

War at sea: Japanese steamer Hirano Maru is torpedoed off the coast of Ireland with the loss of 292 lives.

5

Western Front: End of the Second Battle of Cambrai and the Battle of St. Quentin as Germans pull back to positions along the Suippe River. The main German positions on the Hindenburg Line fall to the Allies.
West of the River Meuse U.S. troops are engaged in fierce fighting.

6

Politics: Yugoslavia declares independence from Austria-Hungary.
In China the civil war becomes official.

Second Battle
of the Marne

JUL

Allied offensive
on Western Front
begins

AUG

Hindenburg Line
positions breached;
Meuse-Argonne
offensive

SEP

Vittorio Veneto
offensive on
Italian Front;
Turkey surrenders

OCT

Armistice on
all fronts

NOV

President Wilson
arrives in Paris;
Yugoslavia created

DEC

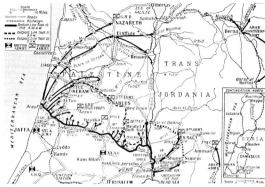

Above left: Turks surrendering in Mesopotamia.

Bottom: Turkish POWs in September 1918.

Russian Revolution: British troops repulse
Bolshevik troops at Seletskaya.

Western Front: Second Battle of Le Cateau
begins as the French attack the Germans at
the Suippe River.

7

Politics: Poland declares independence.
The Turkish government resigns and Izzet
Pasha becomes Grand Vizier.

8

Western Front: Great Allied advance on
20-mile St. Quentin-Cambrai front. Forces
include the British Third and Fourth Armies,
the 30th U.S. Division and French troops.
Successfully drive Germans back three miles.

*Above right: Map of Palestine showing the movements
of British troops during the battle of Meggido,
September 18–23, 1918.*

9

Western Front: Cambrai is taken by the
British and get to within two miles of Le
Cateau. They take 110,000 German prisoners
and 1,200 guns.

10

Russian Revolution: The Russian White (anti-
Bolshevik) commander General Mikhail
Alexeev dies following a heart attack.

Western Front: The British take Le Cateau,
Rouvroy, and Sallaumines.
Germans evacuate the Argonne Forest
following fierce American attacks.

11

Politics: Hungarian premier Alexander
Wekerle resigns.

1918

Strikes and riooting brings Austro-Hungarian Empire to its knees
JAN

Food rationing starts in England
FEB

German spring offensive —the Kaiserschlacht
MAR

Zeebrugge Raid
APR

U.S. forces in action for first time on Western Front at Cantigny
MAY

German offensive held at Battle Chateau-Th /Belleau

Mined British tank.

12

Western Front: End of the Second Battle of Le Cateau follows fighting on the River Selle. End of the Battle for Champagne. General Pershing forms the U.S. Second Army under the command of General Bullard.

14

Politics: In Czechoslovakia a provisional government is formed.

Western Front: Courtrai Offensive. Major Allied attack in Flanders led by the King of the Belgians. They advance five miles. The largest bomb of the war, 1,650lb, is dropped by a Handley Page 0/400 aircraft of the Independent Air Force.

17

Politics: Proclamation in Prague of the Czechoslovakian Republic.

At Agram Yugoslavia announces its independence.

Western Front: Anglo-American attack starts the Battle of the Selle across a nine-mile front. British liberate Lille and enter Douai. Belgians retake Ostend. British advance to the Sambre and Schledt rivers, taking many German prisoners.

18

Western Front: The Belgians reoccupy Zeebrugge and storm Bruges. The Channel coast west of Flanders is liberated.

19

War at sea: German submarines are ordered to return to their bases.

20

Western Front: British cross river Selle.

Second Battle
of the Marne
JUL

Allied offensive
on Western Front
begins
AUG

Hindenburg Line
positions breached;
Meuse-Argonne
offensive
SEP

Vittorio Veneto
offensive on
Italian Front;
Turkey surrenders
OCT

Armistice on
all fronts
NOV

President Wilson
arrives in Paris;
Yugoslavia created
DEC

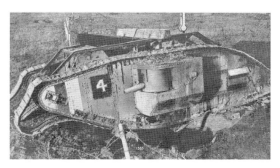

Another British tank that has run over a "plum pudding".

Bottom: British cavalry moving through the streets of Arras.

Cousins and kings. King George (left) greets Albert, King of the Belgians at his HQ in the village of La Panne.

the Vittoria Veneto with some success.

21
War at sea: Germany ceases unrestricted submarine warfare.

22
Western Front: British troops enter Valenciennes.
American troops engaged in fierce fighting on both banks of the Meuse and north of Verdun.

23
Western Front: British push the German line back three miles with a big attack between Le Cateau and Valenciennes. Take Bruay and reach the River Scheldt.

23
Italian Front: Italian Vittorio Veneto Offensive as Italian forces attack Austro-Hungarians in

24
Balkans: On the Southern Front the Third Battle of the Piave begins with a successful Serb advance.

25
Western Front: The Battle of the Selle ends as the British advance between Le Quesnoy and Maing.

26
Middle East: British advanced troops occupy Aleppo and the Turks retreat along the Tigris to Kalaat Shergat.

Politics: General von Ludendorff resigns.

1918

Strikes and riooting brings Austro-Hungarian Empire to its knees
JAN

Food rationing starts in England
FEB

German spring offensive –the Kaiserschlacht
MAR

Zeebrugge Raid
APR

U.S. forces in action for first time on Western Front at Cantigny
MAY

German offensive held at Battle of Chateau-Thi /Belleau
J

The Menin Road in October 1918.

27
Politics: The Austro-Hungarians apply for an armistice. Following von Ludendorff's resignation General Wilhelm Gröner replaces him as deputy Army chief of staff. He authorizes the immediate withdrawal of German forces in France.

28
Balkans: The Tenth and Twelfth Italian Armies advance despite fierce fighting. The Austrians are driven back and the Italians enter Allessio in Albania.

29
United States: German sailors manning the German High Seas Fleet at Jade refuse to obey orders to engage the British fleet for the 'final battle' when they know the war is already lost. When the news spreads to Germany other mutinies follow.

30
Mesopotamia: The Turkish Army on the Tigris surrenders to the British.

Politics: At Mudros Turkey signs an armistice with the Allies. Hostilities cease at noon the following day.

War at sea: The German High Seas Fleet starts to mutiny.

31
Italian Front: On the Southern Front the Austrian commander-in-chief applies to General Diaz for an armistice.

November 1918
German troops withdraw back to Germany as the Central Powers collapse in the face of Allied successes. The outcome is the liberation of France and Belgium and the overthrow of

Second Battle
of the Marne
JUL

Allied offensive
on Western Front
begins
AUG

Hindenburg Line
positions breached;
Meuse-Argonne
offensive
SEP

Vittorio Veneto
offensive on
Italian Front;
Turkey surrenders
OCT

Armistice on
all fronts
NOV

President Wilson
arrives in Paris;
Yugoslavia created
DEC

The British flag rises over Kirkuk on October 25, 1918,

Bottom: Three British dispatch riders on a road through an Alpine gorge on the Italian front narrowly escape the burst of a gas shell.

American troops disembarking onto the quay at Liverpool. The first contingent arrived in autumn 1917.

German and Ausrto-Hungarian monarchies and aristocracies.

1

Politics: The Hungarian National Council declares independence from Austria.
King Boris of Bulgaria abdicates.
Serbian troops reoccupy Belgrade.

War at sea: At Pola in Austria the Austro-Hungarian dreadnought Viribus Unitis is sunk by Italians.

Western Front: Battle of the Sambre begins with a Franco-American advance between the Aisne and Meuse in the Argonne Forest. The attack at Forêt de Bourgogne starts a rapid American advance. The British reach the suburbs of Valenciennes in Belgium.

3

Politics: Austria-Hungary signs an armistice with the Allies. The Yugoslav National Council announce their intention to form a common state with Serbia and Montenegro.

War at sea: Kiel Mutiny. The German fleet mutinies at Kiel following the earlier mutiny of the High Seas Fleet.

4

Politics: Revolution in Hamburg.

Western Front: Sambre Offensive. Huge Anglo-French offensive along a 30-mile front from Valenciennes to the Oise Canal. This is the last major attack by the Allies on the Western Front and it encounters mostly token German resistance. The last intense air combat of the war. The RAF claims 68 enemy aircraft for 60 losses.

181

1918

Strikes and riooting brings Austro-Hungarian Empire to its knees
JAN

Food rationing starts in England
FEB

German spring offensive —the Kaiserschlacht
MAR

Zeebrugge Raid
APR

U.S. forces in action for first time on Western Front at Cantigny
MAY

German offensive held at Battle Chateau-Th/Belleau

Review of French and American in the Vosges.

5

Politics: The Allied Supreme War Council accepts the German armistice terms.

United States: In the U.S., elections for Congress return a republican majority.

7

Politics: The King of Bavaria flees from Munich into exile.

8

Politics: Protracted armistice negotions start. Allies present their ceasefire terms to the Germans in Ferdinand Foch's railway carriage headquarters at Compiègne. Marshal Foch receives German peace delegates — if they refuse the Allies will continue to advance on Germany, disarm and imprison its troops and occupy the left bank of the Rhine.
Prince Max of Baden declares that Germany is beaten and resigns as Chancellor.
The King of Württemberg and Duke Ernest of Brunswick abdicate. In Munich the Provisional National Council's president Kurt Eisner declares the Bavarian Republic.

Western Front: The Allied advance continues: British take Avesnes and Maubeuge. The French and Americans clear the heights east of the Meuse.

9

Politics: Kaiser Wilhelm II of Germany abdicates and with the Crown Prince flees to Holland to live in exile.
Revolution breaks out in Berlin and a provisional socialist coalition is formed.

War at sea: Off Gibralter the British battleship HMS Britannia is torpedoed and sunk: 40 lives are lost.

Second Battle of the Marne
JUL

Allied offensive on Western Front begins
AUG

Hindenburg Line positions breached; Meuse-Argonne offensive
SEP

Vittorio Veneto offensive on Italian Front; Turkey surrenders
OCT

Armistice on all fronts
NOV

President Wilson arrives in Paris; Yugoslavia created
DEC

Sir Hugh Trenchard, commander of the independent air force in France in 1918.

Bottom: US troops from the 7th Infantry Regiment.

The Armistice is signed at Compiègne, November 11, 1918. Foch carries the terms in his briefcase.

10

War at sea: Off the northeast coast of England British mine sweeper Ascot is torpedoed and sunk by a German submarine: 53 lost.

11

Politics: Armistice Day. The Armistice was signed at 5am to come into effect on the eleventh hour, of the eleventh day, of the eleventh month, 1918. This effectively halts the war. The final Treaty of Versailles, is signed on June 28, 1919. Roughly ten million soldiers have been killed and a further ten million civilians died from disease and starvation.

At 10:45am the crew of a 15 Sqn RE.8 observation aircraft landed at Auchy and reported that they had seen no enemy aircraft or anti-aircraft fire.

Abdications across Germany – the Grand Dukes of Hesse, Mecklenberg and Saxe-Weimar; the King of Saxony and the Grand Duke of Oldenburg are deposed. Hungary declares itself a republic.

Western Front: Before dawn the British capture and liberate Mons. End of the Battle of the Sambre.

12

Politics: The terms of the Armistice are published.

13

Politics: The abdication of Emperor Karl of Austria is announced in Vienna.

War at sea: Allied navies occupy Constantinople.

1918

Strikes and rioting brings Austro-Hungarian Empire to its knees
JAN

Food rationing starts in England
FEB

German spring offensive —the Kaiserschlacht
MAR

Zeebrugge Raid
APR

U.S. forces in action for first time on Western Front at Cantigny
MAY

German offensive held at Battle of Chateau-Thi /Belleau

November 21, 1918: Germany's fleet steams towards Britain to surrender . . . (see page 188).

14

Africa: In Northern Rhodesia General von Lettow-Vorbeck and his Schutztruppe (army) surrender at Abercorn to the British.

Politics: In Vienna the Republic of German-Austria is proclaimed. The Czechoslovak National Assembly elects Tomas Masaryk head of state.

16

Politics: Emperor Karl abdicates the throne of Hungary.

Western Front: Allied soldiers begin to move towards Germany.

18

United States: President Wilson announces that he will personally attend the peace conference.

Western Front: Belgian troops enter Antwerp and Brussels to great rejoicing.

19

Politics: The King and Queen of the Belgians return to Antwerp.

21

War at sea: The 'Capitulation of Rosyth' sees the surrender of the German High Seas Fleet. Nine German dreadnoughts, five battlecruisers, seven cruisers, 49 destroyers. They are escorted by HMS Cardiff to anchor off the Firth of Forth by 33 dreadnoughts (including five U.S.) , nine battlecruisers, one carrier, seven squadrons of cruisers and 150 destroyers, in two lines, six miles apart and 15 miles long.
Off Harwich 39 German submarines surrender.

Second Battle of the Marne **JUL**

Allied offensive on Western Front begins **AUG**

Hindenburg Line positions breached; Meuse-Argonne offensive **SEP**

Vittorio Veneto offensive on Italian Front; Turkey surrenders **OCT**

Armistice on all fronts **NOV**

President Wilson arrives in Paris; Yugoslavia created **DEC**

On November 22, 1918, the King and Queen of the Belgians reenter Brussels.

Bottom: US 340mm railway gun in the Argonne. Crew 22; range 20 miles.

People gather outside Buckingham Palace on Armistice Day.

22

Politics: The King and Queen of the Belgians return to Brussels.

23

Politics: At Agram an assembly of southern Slavic states announce the union of all Slavic states in Austria-Hungary together with Serbia and Montenegro to become Yugoslavia.

24

Politics: The Duke of Baden abdicates.

25

Africa: The last German forces in East Africa surrender to the British.

Politics: Marshal Foch enters Strasburg.

26

Russian Revolution: Allied squadrons arrive at Odessa and Sevastopol.

Western Front: The last German troops leave Belgium.

28

Politics: The Kaiser signs the formal deed of abdication.

December 1918

German troops greeted as returning heroes as they march through Berlin.

1

Politics: In Belgrade the Kingdom of Serbs, Croats and Slovenes (Yugoslavia) becomes official.

Strikes and rioting brings Austro-Hungarian Empire to its knees **JAN**

Food rationing starts in England **FEB**

German spring offensive —the Kaiserschlacht **MAR**

Zeebrugge Raid **APR**

U.S. forces in action for first time on Western Front at Cantigny **MAY**

German offensive held at Battle of Chateau-Thierry /Belleau ...

The Supreme War Council of the Allies in session in Versailles discuss armistice terms.

War at sea: Eight more German submarines surrender at Harwich.

Western Front: British Second Army enters Germany between Oudler and Eupen. American forces enter Germany and occupy Trier.

4

United States: President Wilson sails for the Paris Peace Conference aboard the liner George Washington.

9

Western Front: Americans reach the River Rhine.
French enter Mainz.

11

Western Front: American troops occupy Coblenz.

12

Western Front: British troops cross the Rhine and take possession of the Cologne bridgehead.

13

Politics: By mutual agreement the Armistice is prolonged for a month – until 17 January.

Western Front: American troops cross the Rhine and take possession of the Coblenz bridgehead.
President Wilson arrives at Brest, in France. becoming the first U.S. president to travel to Europe while holding office.

14

Politics: Polling day for the British General Election.
President Wilson arrives in Paris.

Second Battle
of the Marne
JUL

Allied offensive
on Western Front
begins
AUG

Hindenburg Line
positions breached;
Meuse-Argonne
offensive
SEP

Vittorio Veneto
offensive on
Italian Front;
Turkey surrenders
OCT

Armistice on
all fronts
NOV

President Wilson
arrives in Paris;
Yugoslavia created
DEC

The boulevards of Paris on Armistice Day.

Bottom: French cavalry enter Strasbourg on November 25, 1918: it had been in German hands since being ceded to Germany in 1871.

28
Politics: Announcement that Lloyd George and his Coalition Government have been returned to power in the general election in Great Britain.

1919
The peace processes lead to treaties designed to ensure World War I is the war to end all wars. In Russia the Civil War continues.

January 1919

12
Paris Peace Conference starts.

25
Peace conference accepts principle of a League of Nations

British forces—in the shape of 28th Brigade of 9th Division—occupy Cologne on December 7, 1918.

February 1919

14
Draft covenant of League of Nations completed

23
Benito Mussolini forms the Fascist Party in Italy.

March 1919

2
The first Communist International meets in Moscow

4
Founding of Comintern (Third International) at Moscow

1918

Strikes and rioting
brings Austro-Hungarian
Empire to its knees
JAN

Food rationing
starts in England
FEB

German spring
offensive
—the Kaiserschlacht
MAR

Zeebrugge Raid
APR

U.S. forces in action
for first time on
Western Front
at Cantigny
MAY

German offensive
held at Battle o
Chateau-Th
/Belleau

The German fleet was scuttled on June 21, 1919. This is Hindenburg.

13
Admiral Kolchak begins his offensive against Bolsheviks in Russian Civil War

14
President Wilson returns to Paris after a month's absence

23
In Milan, Italy, Benito Mussolini founds his Fascist political movement.

April 1919

24
Italian Premier Orlando walks out of peace conference over Fiume issue

May 1919

6
Peace conference disposes of German colonies

7
Treaty of Versailles drafted The German delegation arrives in Paris to sign the peace treaty. They are surprised by the severity of the terms and initially balk at signing.

June 1919

21
German High Seas Fleet scuttled at Scapa Flow on expiration of armistace and before the Treaty of Versailles is signed. Only 1 dreadnought, 3 cruisers and some TBs beached and saved from sinking.

28
Treaty of Versailles signed by Germany and the Allies signed in the Hall of Mirrors at

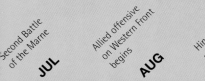

Second Battle of the Marne
JUL

Allied offensive on Western Front begins
AUG

Hindenburg Line positions breached; Meuse-Argonne offensive
SEP

Vittorio Veneto offensive on Italian Front; Turkey surrenders
OCT

Armistice on all fronts
NOV

President Wilson arrives in Paris; Yugoslavia created
DEC

New York greets the news of the Armistice.

French searchlights near Koblenz on the Rhine.

Versaille. The United States signs treaty of guaranty, pledging to defend France in case of an unprovoked attack by Germany.

July 1919

19
Cenotaph is unveiled in London.

August 1919

11
In Germany, the Weimar Constitution is passed into law.

September 1919

10
The Treaty of St Germain en Laye is signed by Austria and the Allies.

October 1919

2
US President Woodrow Wilson suffers a massive stroke, leaving him partially paralyzed.

November 1919
At end of month health officials declare the global Spanish Flu Pandemic over

19
United States Senate fails to ratify Treaty of Versailles.

27
The Treaty of Neuilly is signed by Bulgaria and the Allies.

1918

Strikes and rioting brings Austro-Hungarian Empire to its knees
JAN

Food rationing starts in England
FEB

German spring offensive —the Kaiserschlacht
MAR

Zeebrugge Raid
APR

U.S. forces in action for first time on Western Front at Cantigny
MAY

German offensive held at Battle of Chateau-Thierry /Belleau Th...

British forces—a battalion of the King's Regiment (Liverpool)—enter Lille.

1920

Poland becomes independent as WWI comes to an end. The country was devastated by the war. Approximately one million Poles died. All Polish institutions had to be rebuilt as the country once again formed a nation. The official boundaries are not set until 1923.

January 1920

10

Treaty of Versailles takes effect.

March 1920

19

United States Senate fails to ratify Treaty of Versailles for the second time.

June 1920

4

The Treaty of Trianon is signed by Hungary and the Allies.

August 1920

10

The Treaty of Sévres is signed by the former Ottoman Empire and the Allies.

1921

August 1920

24–29

United States signs separate peace treaties with Germany, Austria, and Hungary.

Although almost obliterated by enemy bombardments, Ypres was the only important Belgian town not to fall to the Germans, despite being the scene of three of the costliest battles of the war. Postwar the city would have to be completely rebuilt.

Bonn is occupied by the British, December 14, 1918.

British graves at Abbeville tended by members of the WRACs.